All the
Lives I
Want

All the Lives I Want

*Essays About My Best Friends Who
Happen to Be Famous Strangers*

ALANA MASSEY

GRAND CENTRAL
PUBLISHING

NEW YORK   BOSTON

Grand Central Publishing
Hachette Book Group
1290 Avenue of the Americas, New York, NY 10104
grandcentralpublishing.com
twitter.com/grandcentralpub

First Edition: February 2017

Grand Central Publishing is a division of Hachette Book Group, Inc.
The Grand Central Publishing name and logo is a trademark of
Hachette Book Group, Inc.

The Hachette Speakers Bureau provides a wide range of authors for
speaking events. To find out more, go to www.hachettespeakersbureau.com
or call (866) 376-6591.

Library of Congress Cataloging-in-Publication Data

Names: Massey, Alana, author.
Title: All the lives I want : essays about my best friends who happen to be
   famous strangers / Alana Massey.
Description: First edition. | New York : Grand Central Publishing, 2017.
Identifiers: LCCN 2016023351 | ISBN 9781455565887 (hardback) |
   ISBN 9781455565870 (ebook)
Subjects: LCSH: Women—United States—Social conditions—21st century. |
   Celebrities—United States—History—21st century. | BISAC: SOCIAL
   SCIENCE / Essays.
Classification: LCC HQ1421 .M345 2017 | DDC 305.420973—dc23 LC record
available at https://lccn.loc.gov/2016023351

ISBNs: 978-1-4555-6588-7 (hardcover), 978-1-4555-6587-0 (ebook)

Printed in the United States of America

LSC-C

10 9 8 7 6 5 4 3 2 1

For my sister Nova, the first star I ever wanted to be.

We realized that the version of the world they rendered for us was not the world they really believed in.

—Jeffrey Eugenides, *The Virgin Suicides*

Contents

CONTENTS

All the
Lives I
Want

Being Winona; Freeing Gwyneth

On the Limitations of Our Celebrity "Type"

I SHOULD HAVE FORESEEN THAT things between James and me would end in violent chaos on the night of my twenty-ninth birthday when he, my best friend Phoebe, and I were each contemplating who our No. 1 most bangable celebrity was. Phoebe and I had declared our respective loves for Harry Styles and John Malkovich. Then James said, "You know, I've always had a soft spot for Gwyneth Paltrow."

"Gwyneth *Paltrow*?" I repeated back to him in horror.

"Yeah, there's something about her. I don't know what it is!" And in that moment, every thought or daydream I'd ever had about our potential future together filled with broad-smiled children, adopted cats, and phenomenal sex evaporated. Because there is no future with a Gwyneth man when you're a Winona woman, particularly a Winona in a world made for Gwyneths.

Just as Phoebe and I wax poetic about which celebrities we'd let impregnate us, we've also devoted considerable time to the ones we feel our lives most resemble. It is from this game that I developed my "Winona in a world made for Gwyneths" complex. This theory positions these onetime best friends as two distinct categories of white women who are conventionally attractive but whose public images exemplify dramatically different lifestyles and worldviews. The interesting thing I've found about asking women whether they're Gwyneths or Winonas is that self-assessments are almost universally in concert with external assessments. I've seen dramatic escalations when a self-identified Charlotte was told by friends that she was a Miranda, but for the most part, Winonas know that they're Winonas and Gwyneths know that they're Gwyneths. What's more interesting is that people are usually happy about it, too.

One lives a messy but somehow more authentic life that is at once exciting and a little bit sad. The other appears to have a life so sufficiently figured out as to be both enviable and mundane. Gwyneth Paltrow is, of course, the latter. She has always represented a collection of tasteful but safe consumer reflexes more than she's reflected much of a real personality. I imagine that she writes the GOOP newsletter, her laughably out-of-touch dispatch about vegetables and fashion, wearing overpriced clothes in colors like "camel" and scowling at her staff. That is, when she's not referring to Billy Joel as "William"[1] and seeking nannies who know ancient Greek and play at least two instruments.[2]

For girls of my generation who were awkward or a little bit strange, Winona Ryder was both relatable and aspirational. The few recorded interviews she's done reveal that she is a bottomless well of uncool and discomfort.[3] She stumbles over metaphors and laughs sincerely at bad jokes. She is also a movie star who is unreasonably beautiful, but there was always a sense that she still belonged to the Island of Misfit Toys.

She epitomized the Mall Goth ethic *and* aesthetic in *Beetlejuice* long before Hot Topic was mass-producing the look, and in *Heathers*, she enacted high school revenge fantasies long before *Mean Girls* was either a movie or PG shorthand for "fucking bitches." In the '90s, she did her grungiest best as the Generation X poster child in *Reality Bites* but never met a corset she didn't like and came at us with *The Age of Innocence* and *Dracula*. I can't even talk about *Little Women*, because I'll just start crying about the fact that I'm not currently sitting under a pile of kittens and sisters.

Then there's her romantic life, which reads like a who's who of my sexual awakening. Val Kilmer, Rob Lowe, Christian Slater, Beck, David Duchovny, and a bunch of indie rock stars who are probably still in love with her. Gwyneth had a shorter and more predictable list of conventional handsome dudes, including Brad Pitt and Ben Affleck, before she married Chris Martin. But Winona's love stories seem like a series of elaborate fan fictions come to life for the charming and constantly bewildered pixie of a person. And I'm sure I don't need to remind anyone that Johnny Depp wore her name on his bicep when he was still starring in daring, quirky films instead of predictable Tim Burton cash cows.

But just as Winona's legendary series of whirlwind romances wouldn't last forever, neither would mine with James. Many of the tabloid stories reported that she was devastated by her relationships ending. I realize that celebrity breakup synopses often cast the woman as the sad sack who can't catch a man with a net because it's a neat narrative. But, good god, it was also my narrative and I needed a hero.

As interesting as I always found her love life, though, it was still her personality and talent that drew me in. Rumor has it that Winona had the script for *Shakespeare in Love* and that Gwyneth saw it at her house and surreptitiously sought out the producers to get the role that landed her the Oscar.[4] It is one of many Hollywood whispers that Gwyneth is not so sweet as she presents. And the long list of "best friends" she seems to have had over the years (Winona, Madonna, Tracy Anderson, Beyoncé) looks more than a little opportunistic.

It would have all been fine for Winona, because she was starring in the adaptation of *Girl, Interrupted*. Except that turned out to be the movie that would actually work to catapult Angelina Jolie to stardom and earn *her* an Oscar. And then came her 2001 arrest for shoplifting. The incident revealed a more complicated, less whimsical Winona; she was actually unwell, an inconvenient reality better dealt with through punch lines than public sympathy. And while male performers have gone on violent and destructive benders and bounced back in the time since that incident, Winona's reputation has never fully recovered.

I loved Winona as a kid but grew even more affectionate for her in my late teens and early adulthood, long after the "Free Winona" T-shirts had cycled out of ironic fashion. She was wide-eyed and wistful but managed to find love from time to time anyway. I felt I could reasonably aspire to that.

Like many men before him, James was more capable of getting into relationships than he had let on, just not with me. He was leaving me for someone else, and when he said, "I know you want me to mess this up with her, but I won't," I paused a moment before speaking. "No, but I hope that she chooses someone over you," I told him, with a suddenly regained composure. He went to leave and with my back turned to him, I said, "I hope she chooses someone over you *twice.*" My voice cracked as I delivered these last words, adding to the drama of the whole encounter and clearly cutting him to the core. I sat there devastated, in a pile of my own tears without a sister or a kitten in sight, but at least I'd delivered a line to remember me by.

An exceedingly quick search through Facebook revealed the identity of his new girlfriend. And there she was. A total. Fucking. Gwyneth. In addition to long blond hair, she had earnest gratitude posts featuring all the superboring emoticons. She posted photos of sunsets and filtered her selfies to hell and back with Instagram. On Facebook, she posted photos of a white SUV and nights out at a club. I couldn't see her feet, but I joked cruelly to a friend, "She's probably wearing espadrilles." A quick Google search brought up a photo of her cheerfully giving what appears to be a presentation about industrial label makers. In sharp contrast to my online life, a collection of mostly drily despairing essays for online magazines and unfiltered Twitter jokes, her entire digital footprint accumulated into a collection of safe consumer reflexes more than a personality.

And though I am easily given to fits of envy, I looked at her life and couldn't find a single thing to covet. I was a haphazardly medicated bipolar twenty-nine-year-old stripper and I didn't want *anything* she had. I felt the way I imagined Winona felt surveying the foreign landscape of GOOP, laughing incredulously at the appeal of such dull aspirations but also completely and utterly alone.

I attached actively to my sense of Winona-ness in the months that followed the breakup. I shared the observation about how seeing this woman's profile was how Winona probably felt if she ever read GOOP and left out the sad part at the end about being alone so that it could be a joke. If I was in on the joke, it couldn't hurt me.

Although I originally thought being unchosen was my moment where Gwyneth snatched up *Shakespeare in Love*, I realize now that her getting James was less like getting an award-winning movie script and more like getting that scary VHS tape from *The Ring* that eventually ruins your life. I've instead come to see the whole experience as my moment on a surveillance camera in Saks Fifth Avenue. It was the episode in which the Manic Pixie Dream Girl was revealed to be the Depressive Witch Nightmare Woman that she was all along. It brought to life my sadness and desperation outside the vacuum where being mentally ill was a fascinating quirk that had no potential to create real consequences. I was breakable and broken and would not be confined to the narrative that James, and the long line of men whose footsteps he had followed in, had in mind for me.

The mythology I built around Winona Ryder saw me through heavyheartedness and I am grateful to have had her by my metaphorical side. But the deeper I dove into the archive of headlines about Winona, the more closely I read her interviews, and the more distance I got from my own postbreakup myopia, the more I realized that I had done Winona the same disservice that had been done to me. I had made her an avatar that represented my own suffering and refused to register both stated facts and notable omissions from the record that might suggest otherwise. The public discourse about Winona had trapped her as the long-suffering girl, and I was in collusion with it. The decision to actively disengage from that way of looking at Winona made me sympathetic to an unlikely ally: Gwyneth Paltrow.

Giving Winona back her full humanity meant giving it back to Gwyneth, too. So as humiliated as I was to be left for someone I identified as a "Gwyneth" before, my thoughts about her turned mostly into hopes that she's safe and happy.

Because the thing about Gwyneth Paltrow that James couldn't articulate is that there's *not really anything about her*. Or at least there's not anything about her public image that is especially unique or controversial. She's a safe canvas onto which others can project their own desires, including the defiant and childish desire to define oneself as against the things she is alleged to stand for. I know very well that the woman James left me for is not an empty collection of label makers and earnest Facebook posts, just as I know that Gwyneth Paltrow is not her terrible newsletter.

Her breakup with Chris Martin was widely mocked in the press for being identified as a "conscious uncoupling," as though she could not bear to have anything so human and messy as what it was: a divorce. For months after the split, rumors flew that Gwyneth was terrified that details of their marriage would emerge, that the perfect filter she had chosen for the world to see her through would be ripped off to reveal all the blemished and broken parts. Such forms of protected and limited self-projection are calculated and intentional. And that seems like its own kind of solitude. Despite whatever loneliness, real or imagined, Gwyneth experiences, she seems steadfast in her commitment to being in on the joke in a way that I know well.

I turned thirty the following June, the age Winona was when the shoplifting scandal went down. As I stared down the birthday, I feared that I'd be forced to turn the corner from wide-eyed and wistful to just sad and sick. And when you rely heavily on celebrities like Winona Ryder to make sense of your life, it is easy to stare down your early thirties as the period of darkness and uncertainty following a fallout. But just as I had clumsily retrofitted my life story with all the telltale signs of being a classic Winona, it was preemptive to fear my thirties. Though I write this from the earliest stages of them, they have so far contained an amount of joy and love thus far unprecedented in my life.

The truth about the women who are forced to play these interesting chapters is that they are doing so in the memoirs of men who never deserved them. That the really good story, the story worth telling, has been theirs all along. They just have to survive to tell it. And that's what Winona did. In the fall of 2014, just a few months after the end with James, Winona became the face of the Rag & Bone fashion line and was featured in a series of promotional videos for the launch. She doesn't appear to have aged a day since 1990, and she smiles through red lipstick as she plays arcade games at Coney Island. The arcade is dimly lit and deserted except for her. But she seems perfectly content to make goofy faces and have her own fun, telling herself a bad joke that no one else can hear, and laughing and laughing.

Public Figures

Britney's Body Is Everybody's

WHEN PEOPLE ASK ME HOW much I weigh, they are often looking for a measure of distance more than a measure of weight. They want to know my weight in pounds, of course, but at the heart of so many inquiries about the weight of a small woman is a desire to know the difference between their bodies and mine. They want to know the distance between these two countries we occupy and the difference in area. As I write this, I weigh 110 pounds. It is a number that I am not uncomfortable with, but I prefer to be from one pound to four pounds lighter, between 106 and 109. The circles on the six and the nine are deceptive roundness, seeing as the body they represent is mostly defined by straight lines at this weight. The zeros in the middle of the number serve as numerical thigh gaps: a space to house the coveted nothing that I hunger in the direction of. But my eating disorder is a pathology that gives significance to arbitrary figures, both embodied shapes and numerical ones.

Men often register low weights as normal. Their standard calibrations for the weight of petite women is between 100 and 115 pounds, average ones 115 to 125, and tall ones 125 to 135. These men are completely wrong, of course. But women, too, have a hard time adjusting for height and width to understand how another woman can appear slight but bear a substantial weight or how others can appear so ample but register on the scales at smaller numbers. Further exacerbating the disorientation we experience when faced with other people's statistics that do not match our internal calibrations of them is the preponderance of celebrity programming featuring hypothesized weights and sizes for famous bodies. Exact weights litter fitness and celebrity magazines that seem off somehow but always carry the weight of our judgments, and an internal subtraction problem, to determine our proximity to their shapes. Weighing fewer than 100 pounds indicates too much weight lost, weighing more than 150 pounds indicates a calamitous embarrassment, and weighing over 200 pounds is nothing short of a mortal sin.

I went from small to smaller in the year 2013, after having spent the two years prior hopping between average and the bigger side of little. I have a clear memory of reading *Shape* magazine's Britney Spears cover story that summer in a nail salon and realizing that for the first time since I became aware of Britney existing, I weighed substantially less than her. The subheadline claimed that Britney was "fitter and more fabulous than ever" before detailing her workout routine.[1] That same year, RadarOnline published a slideshow of female celebrities and their weights, some estimated by fitness experts and several culled from a website called Whattheyreallyweigh.com, presumably owned and operated by a deeply happy human being.

But the most frequent place these numbers appear is on the covers of magazines during the annual shame parade that tabloids put famous women through during the summer. The headlines are always some variation of "The Best and Worst Bikini Bodies of the Summer!" The graininess of the collection of candid photos of celebrities at the beach betrays that these images were taken from afar and likely without the knowledge or consent of the celebrity therein. The result is that the featured celebrities are often in the middle of play or halfway through speaking a sentence in these images. Their mouths appear agape and their chins doubled up. And these lists are always incomplete, of course. Not every celebrity goes to the beach during the summer, and certainly not all of them are captured by photographers when they do. But the high volume of celebrities living by the coast in Los Angeles makes the list reasonably robust. And though these images are not taken with their consent, there is always an element of intent written into the copy that surrounds them. Unlike the Victoria's Secret catalog, these images were not posed, and they presumably went largely untouched by the wands of Photoshop, but intentionality is breathed into each picture. Thin and shapely women are always said to be "flaunting" or "showing off" their bikini bodies by simply appearing in public. Those who don't fit within the narrow definition of *perfection* in a given year are "letting it all hang out." A private citizen might be able to take legal action against the offending photographers and the publications that hire them for the privacy violation, but being an entertainer generally means the forfeiture of such an option. Theirs are public figures in every sense of the word.

I rarely purchase these magazines. It is not because I am ashamed of my predilection for gawking at famous flesh but because I feel it would draw attention to my own body. I fear that looking at other bodies would magnify the existence of mine, making me somehow more material than I had been before. But when they were available in the piles of reading materials at nail salons, I would pick them up and feign defeat at the selection, as if I were positively *beleaguered* by some duty to read it. At drugstores with self-service kiosks where the magazines are situated directly next to the machines, I would pick up a copy and swipe the bar code across the scanner in one motion. Once I had the tasteless contraband in my hands, I skipped directly to the section of the magazine where the selections for the "best" bikini bodies were printed. I marveled at how symmetry of muscle and bone in the legs could be as striking as symmetry in the face. I wondered how abdomens could be exercised to so precise a point that they were completely flat but showed no visible muscle definition that might masculinize the effect even slightly.

There are a handful of mainstays that one can expect to find in these magazines year in and year out. Charlize Theron and Jessica Biel both make regular appearances among the best in bikini bodies. Their relentless athleticism makes their bodies appear free of the cellulite that plagues 90 percent of adult women, as beauty magazines are always quick to remind us when we seek out cures for this blight. There are other celebrities who remain in constant rotation on either side of the list because they have gained and lost weight. Nicole Richie was despised for having the audacity to appear on television and not hate herself when she was heavier, as she was later despised for losing a dramatic amount of weight. Jessica Simpson incurred similar wrath for her flagrant refusal to stay thin while *gestating a human*.

Jessica Simpson was the least famous third of a trifecta whose bodies I grew up gazing at alongside an American public that was absolutely rabid for opportunities to scrutinize them. The other two were Christina Aguilera and the legendary Miss Britney Spears, of course. These women came into public life as girls, barely out of puberty and eager to please a public that demanded they be pleasant or face extreme consequences. It was Britney's famous midriff that led the charge of sexualized teen pop stars into lives in the late 1990s with "...Baby One More Time," an anthem that remains nonsensical nearly twenty years after its debut while its accompanying video grows more iconic. Christina entered the public consciousness singing, "My body's saying 'Let's go,' but my heart is saying, 'No,'" on the hit "Genie in a Bottle." Whether it was prescience or accident that a pop star's heart would be considered separate from her body, I am not sure. Then there was Jessica Simpson, who emerged at the tail end of the 1990s as the wholesome response to Christina and Britney but whose own father famously told *GQ* in 2004, "Jessica never tries to be sexy. She just is sexy. If you put her in a T-shirt or you put her in a bustier, she's sexy in both. She's got double D's! You can't cover those suckers up!"[2] But while Christina and Jessica have been given opportunities to respond gracefully to their detractors, there seems to be no rest for the body of Britney.

It was Britney whose performance of "Oops!...I Did It Again" at the 2000 MTV Video Music Awards made history, when the only thing that could upstage the rhinestone-studded nude pants and bustier she wore was the incredible fitness of the body that wore it. I recall watching the VMAs and envying the tautness and smooth tan of her figure, then envying her twice over when boys at school the next day recalled its perfection. More than once that day, a boy declared, "Her body is *insane*." It was an apt description: Maintaining that particular ratio of muscle tone to fat while retaining some level of feminine curves requires round-the-clock diligence, an obsessive single-mindedness, and a kind of madness that I have little confidence these boys knew or cared about.

When Britney married young and began having children, her weight gains and losses became a sport that has not since receded from the public imagination. After Britney's second son was born in 2006, *People* published a workout and diet regimen that she was allegedly adhering to in order to lose her pregnancy weight; however, this was unsubstantiated by Britney or anyone on her team. *People* then had the audacity to shame her for its rigor. The regimen involved the standard fare of "secrets" that are not secret at all: six small meals in lieu of three hardy ones, cardiovascular exercise, and removal of white flour and processed sugar. Before launching into the piece, there is the benevolent caveat: "The last thing a brand new mom should be concerned about is weight loss. This is the time to take care of your baby and yourself. The weight will come off later. Even celebrities whose job it is to look good should keep this in mind. Your baby will only be a baby once." It takes just one sentence for the writer to go off script. The narrative goes from a focus on new mothers taking care of themselves to revealing that this is actually all about a neglected infant whose mother resides in one of the world's most frequently dissected bodies. "We are worried about the message that this sends to new moms, that it's safe to exercise like this following a birth and that this kind of weight loss in a short period of time is normal," they write, judgment oozing from so brief an admonition.[3]

It is common to say that "the years were unkind" to a person, but in the case of Britney Spears, it is irresponsible to blame nonsentient time for unkindness when there was a wealth of people being unkind to her. From her harrowing breakdown to her ongoing weight struggles, the tabloids do not relent and do not forget. In the lower-brow selection of tabloids that report on the weight of celebrities, one statement that follows women struggling with their weight around more than any other is "She got her body back." Here you'll find near-constant Britney coverage. But barring any transcendent out-of-body experiences, these women were never separated from their bodies. They've occupied them across various weights. This phrase is not about a woman getting back something she lost as much as it is about our approval that she has returned to something we want her to be. What is meant by this phrase is "*We* got her body back." We got the body we felt entitled to. In the case of Britney, that is the impossibly lean and limber body of a teenage girl, a body that was enthusiastically characterized as "insane."

The public consumption of Britney did not stop at her figure. The media and those of us who consumed it were obsessed with her sexualities, with a particularly pathological focus on her claim to be a virgin. Though Fred Durst of Limp Bizkit most crudely detailed exactly how she was not a virgin on *The Howard Stern Show*, even the most sophisticated critics couldn't help but indulge in Britney hymen mythology. A profile of Britney by Chuck Klosterman that appeared in *Esquire* in 2003 is now downright painful to read. In it, not a single song or album name from her catalog appears, while no less than seven references are made to the fact that she was not wearing pants at the photo shoot where they met to interview. It is a labored but ultimately unsuccessful attempt to make the case that Britney is "not so much a person as she is an *idea*, and the idea is this: you can want everything, so long as you get nothing." Obviously, "Britney is the naughtiest good girl of all time." But what makes her so different from previous incarnations of jailbait purity—Tiffany, Brooke Shields, Annette Funicello, et alia—is her "abject unwillingness to recognize that this paradox exists at all." He recounts asking her why she dresses provocatively, noting her present attire reveals "three inches of her inner thigh, her entire abdomen, and enough cleavage to choke a musk ox," but not reminding readers that they're at a photo shoot that doesn't involve pants. It is a cloying interview where she protests at his questions about her feelings about starring in men's sexual fantasies but he pushes her on it anyway, dissatisfied with her refusal to be salacious.[4] Britney does not own the truth about her own feelings, nor does she own her own body from this vantage point, because the public mistakes their all-consuming need for Britney as her desire to be consumed this way.

For the first several years of my adult-sized life, I was an American size 4. It is a size that sounds small but means average and felt huge, especially among peers whose size 0s casually hung off them throughout college. Though my envy migrated from teen pop stars to couture models, the specters of Britney's former perfection and her fall from grace remained in my periphery. It still does. When I shrank to size 0 and later a 00 and then to a 000 when J.Crew introduced the size in 2014, I looked at all of these famous bodies with a different set of eyes, both literally and figuratively. My already large hazel eyes had been made more prominent on a face lacking fat, where they protruded more hungrily and took up more real estate. Figuratively, I look at the bodies that were considered so perfect and realize the precariousness of that perfection as I struggle to maintain a size that is attractively delicate without being repulsively bony.

I have been called "perfect" far more often when I am below a healthy body weight than when I am at a normal one. I have heard and read the word "insane" to compliment my body and am driven mad by it. I have heard my body referred to as a "buffet of bones" and a "little rib buffet" by two very different men. The idea of being actual meat is at once thrilling and infuriating: Being eaten bears the promise of no longer existing physically at all. It is when I am caught up in these feelings that young Britney is instructive. Though it was the 2000 performance at the VMAs that cemented Britney's body in my mind as the most aspirational, a perhaps more famous display of her figure was on the cover of *Rolling Stone* in 1999. She was a rising teen sensation giving what seem to be safe, canned answers about ambition and music in her childhood home, but there is a single moment that feels especially off script. In response to questions about romantic rumors, her reply is printed as " 'I have,' she says, *'no feelings at all.'* "[5] I read those italics and see the heart of the story, the crack in her voice well before she cracked. It is a well-rehearsed girl who has been all but mandated to be consumed without biting back, not to cause a fuss so that people will fuss over her. It is a sad surrender but one that makes her queen in the country of popular culture. I wonder now if she knew just how heavy that would feel.

Run the World

Amber Rose in the Great Stripper Imaginary

O
H, I LIKE TO DANCE to everything!" is a lie I've told
many times but that I regretted telling only once.
It was a canned response I'd give to men in VIP rooms as
they edged closer to asking personal questions. We would
be halfway into a conversation that I wanted desperately out
of, often about a shrill and unreasonable wife at home (she
was likely neither) or a half-formed treatise about how he
understood the complexities of my emotional labor and erotic
capital (he definitely understood neither). A new song on the
speakers was a welcome reprieve from indulging this nonsense
to change the subject to topics more favorable to maintaining
my composure. The undiscerning but somehow charming
musical tastes of the impossibly buoyant persona I inhabited
in those darkened rooms was such a subject. There was no
way to talk more substantively about the music playing in the

club without betraying that I was thinking about these songs not as external units of sound to be consumed but as stories to inhabit more perfectly.

I would halt a moment and shift my eyes upward, that strange human habit whereby we think we can look in the direction of surround sound to better recognize melodies whose names elude us. "Oh my god, I love this song!" I would declare, conjuring enthusiasm and changing to a position less conducive to his sharing untoward or uninteresting secrets. It would be impolite for him to completely redirect the conversation back to his tale of domestic adversity and so he would attempt to direct it back to me, asking my favorite song to dance to. "Oh, I like to dance to everything!" I would report with a shrug and a grin. I would wrap my legs tighter around his middle, lean toward his body, and refuse eye contact, not as a matter of detachment but because my focus was now elsewhere, on the song I purported to love so much.

In October 2014, I told this lie to the DJ at a strip club in midtown Manhattan. The declaration was less an exclamation point than a shrugging politeness for which there is no punctuation. I was about to audition for their night shift. It was a reluctant and defeated return. It always is for me. In August, my ex had launched a brief but terrifying scorched-earth policy against me and my reputation. The social worker with whom I'd spoken told me that it was possible he would show up at the club where I worked in order to humiliate me and instructed me not to go in to work if I could avoid it. I stayed home from a few shifts, he fortunately left the state.

I just never went back. It was the fourth time in my stripping career when I was truly convinced that this was it, my last night was really behind me.

Then I found myself with a $900 prescription to fill and no insurance to soften the blow. I have fallen victim to memory lapses during manic episodes that make me think I can live without antipsychotic medications, but I was blessed to be in a depressive state at the time. Another winter approached and I was sad to stubbornly be living the life into which I was born. I felt death lingering near the ends of my own fingertips. And with an in-box full of rejections and silence from the seven hundred jobs for which I had applied in the previous year, I knew that the shortest distance between me and $900 was the length of a hot-pink nylon-and-spandex minidress covering a quarter of my body.

And because it is my custom to present myself to managers as relentlessly, foolishly cheerful at club auditions, I told the DJ that I liked to dance to everything with a shrug and a grin, aware that the manager was still within earshot. An audition generally consists of two songs: the first with the dress on and the second with the dress half off. Even when it is just an audition, management does not like to interrupt the otherwise ongoing show, and so auditioners are called to the stage by their performer names as if they already work at the club. "Lane, can I get Lane to the main stage?" he overinflected into his microphone. I dutifully climbed the three steps on the side of the stage and helped down the girl who had just finished, as is customary if she is clearly struggling with the height of her shoes and the cash haphazardly tucked into her G-string and you're not a total fucking bitch. I held the pole in preparation.

I recognized the first few chords immediately and swayed briefly to the familiar guitar curlicue, but I was certain the song had been played by accident and would be corrected immediately. Guitar strings buzzing gave way to a synthetic arpeggio, however, and it became clear that the DJ had every intention of playing this song. A voice emerged from the stale air to say, "Welcome to your life / There's no turning back," as if reciting from my own punitive internal monologue. The song was "Everybody Wants to Rule the World" by Tears for Fears, an anthemic pop song that has occupied countless minds for hours on end with its catchiness and inspired approximately zero erections with its massive dearth of sexual references.

"Help me make the most of freedom and of pleasure / Nothing ever lasts forever / Everybody wants to rule the world." I heard the lyrics with a pitiless clarity and took notice of musical elements that I had never been in the custom of detecting. "Everybody Wants to Rule the World" contains not one but two guitar solos, for example. And while there are plenty of guitar solos that one can strip to, Tears for Fears is not responsible for any of them.

The song ultimately doesn't work because it is sung in the first person; there is no romantic or sexual object to inhabit. There is only the dreaded occupation of inhabiting the song's first-person narrative coming to terms with the destructiveness of war. But I am reasonably seasoned at these auditions at this point and get the job anyway. And so I start again the process of embodying the narratives of other imaginary women with whom I cross paths on the club sound track.

Some songs are famously about individuals. "In Your Eyes" by Peter Gabriel is about Rosanna Arquette's eyes. "You Oughta Know" by Alanis Morissette is about Dave Coulier's apparent predilection for oral sex in theaters, among other things. "Heart-Shaped Box" by Nirvana is about Courtney Love's...you know. I have never heard any of these songs in a strip club. What I have heard far more often are songs directed at an unidentified "you" or about an unidentified "her" and subsequently let the predominantly male voices singing them inform how I might make use of their words for my own financial benefit.

A famously popular strip club song is "Closer" by Nine Inch Nails, sometimes delicately referred to as the "I wanna fuck you like an animal" song. The song is rotten to the core, but its lyrical simplicity makes it a favorite. I often wonder to whom it was directed. What incredible creature prompted such debased carnal desires in Trent Reznor? Who simultaneously made him desire animal coitus but also reportedly brought him "closer to God"? On more than one occasion onstage and on the strip club floor, I was that person, responding to the song as if it were being sung to me. I danced in a way that was aloof but accessible, that demanded customer effort in a way some men loved and others profoundly despised. Other times I was Reznor, not quite singing along but signaling enough desire with my eyes that the man whose lap I sat in would upgrade to a private room, where we were mercifully spared such graphic lyrics, as "Closer" was over. I hated dancing to this song in the club because I loved it in my personal life. I hated sharing feigned animal desire even for a few minutes. A song that had felt like mine became about so many men and about me and about every person in the club. It lost the particular smell of the Lower ·East Side apartment where it was true; it ended without the pleased sigh of one man's particular climax as he hit the pillow in 2008. I made thousands of dollars dancing as if I were the woman at the center of that song, but I lost a lot to it, too.

One of the best songs specifically about stripping is by Chris Brown, though admitting as much is heresy in my current social circle. The now infamous episode in which he assaulted Rihanna and left contusions on her face remains an open wound to many women. I suspect this is often the case for people who have witnessed only the physical of domestic violence in that particular event. I detest Brown's violence and his apparent refusal to accept the consequences, but only as much as I detest plenty of powerful, famous men whose violence was not as well documented in a public spectacle.

When I first heard a song by Chris Brown while working, it was after 3 a.m., and I and the woman on the second stage exchanged exasperated sighs that we were continuing the charade that men in New York City strip clubs give half a shit about our pole-dancing skills. I saw Brown's name appear on the TV screens that hang in the corners of the club and momentarily imagined the two of us refusing to dance in solidarity against him. But rebellion is the luxury of the paid, and neither of us were especially well paid that night.

In "Strip," Brown's voice is beautiful and his demands are simple. "Girl I just wanna see you strip right now 'cause it's late," he sings. He is the perfect customer. He does not want to know why you work at the club, when you get off, if he can see you later. He does not tell you that he never spends time in "places like this," nor does he suggest that you leave such places entirely without offering some alternative but equally lucrative position to you. He just wants to see you strip. The customer with this demand is the great relief in a job plagued by men who demand so much more than what your title describes. They ask so often that you strip off more than your clothes, but also the character you're playing. They ask that you answer their questions and that you love them for no reason other than the fascinating beat of their own unremarkable hearts.

"Shine bright like a diamond," Rihanna whispers in a song that I loved to dance to and that men seemed to feel ambivalent toward. Rihanna repeats herself sometimes twice, sometimes three times in the song to make certain we have heard her instructions. When I have been onstage for "Diamonds," it has prompted me to look upward at the spotlights, obeying the command recorded years ago and far away, as if Rihanna were presently watching from the sound booth. It is a romantic song, but I've always thought of it as a song directed at a distressed friend by another, assuring her that she is more treasured than she can presently imagine. This is likely because I have used it that way. I would repeat the song's central command in a deadpan voice to work friends on breaks and after shifts, smoking cigarettes and making grandiose proclamations about the big things we had in store for our impending windfalls. I don't know if I said these things because I believed them to be true or because I wanted them to be true, but I don't see those two places as that far from each other anymore.

In one club where I worked, all the girls had to line up on the main stage at the start of the shift and have our names called out one by one as we stepped forward and showed off. It felt like part beauty pageant, part Westminster dog show. It was not uncommon for them to play anthems of empowered womanhood during this interlude, a reminder of how much we all wanted to be there. Songs like "Independent Women II" by Destiny's Child, "LoveGame" by Lady Gaga, and "Bad Girls" by M.I.A. appeared often, while an occasional lament like "Just a Girl" by No Doubt would sneak in that I took for a gentle nod from the DJ that he knew no one working in the club especially wanted to be there.

Once they played "Run the World (Girls)" by Beyoncé, a song that didn't get its fair due as a feminist anthem or as a world-class banger in general. The song was met with criticism on its release, mostly because there is a worldwide committee of curmudgeonly old-guard feminists who refuse to accept Beyoncé as a leader or as one of their own. It was critiqued secondarily because of claims that women do not, in fact, run the world. I think often of this song in contrast to "Everybody Wants to Rule the World" and how Beyoncé was right, as she often is, even when she doesn't always mean to be. Girls run the world in the sense that they perform the invisible and unappreciated labors that keep the world on its axis. That is different from doing what everyone wants to do, which is rule the world. We don't speak of world leaders who *run* countries but of world leaders who *rule* countries. Running a thing is to toil in tedious and uncredited roles; ruling a thing is to hold dominion over it enough that little toil is required. I am glad I heard the song only once in the context of the club, so as not to be driven mad by the grim reality of its literal interpretation. In the light of day and off the clock, not surrounded by the glaring differences of who it is that rules and who it is that runs that were made evident by our coarse exchanges, the song is partially salvaged.

"You Be Killin' 'Em" by Fabolous is the only song I ever cared enough about to request. The upbeat hip-hop celebration of female beauty and power was something of a personal anthem for years. The lyrics on their own might read like a litany of cheesy pickup lines, but accompanied by its urgent and danceable beat, it is a song you can run the fuck out of some errands to. The hook alone contains four compliments to the woman at whom it is directed: "You what's up girl, ain't gotta ask it / I dead 'em all now, I buy the caskets / They should arrest you or whoever dressed you / Ain't gon' stress you, but I'm a let you know / Girl you be killin' 'em / You be killin' 'em." This woman whose appeal is so all-encompassing is rare in any genre, but what is especially remarkable is that her ruthless ambition and apparent materialism are considered attractive.

Several small televisions hung from the ceiling playing the songs' music videos and lighting up the otherwise dark corners of the establishment's main room. I assumed they were primarily for the entertainment of men who had been dragged to the club by friends and needed refuge in something to look at besides the men they knew being reduced to ATMs by an army of scantily clad women. They were also a helpful distraction from the crawl through the first and last hours of dead shifts. More than just giving us something to focus on when there were no customers, they were windows to a world outside the club made glossy and bright by the commonly used palettes and filters of music video aesthetics. Despite being in heavy rotation on my personal playlists, I saw the video for "You Be Killin' 'Em" during the one and only time I danced to it for work.

Taking the title of the song quite literally, Amber Rose plays Fabolous's love interest while living a double life as an assassin. Interspersed with scenes of the two in romantic situations are scenes of Amber wearing disguises and murdering what appears to be an assortment of mobsters of the nouveau riche variety. At the end of the video, Fabolous answers a knock at the door while Amber is in the bathtub and is greeted by several members of law enforcement bearing warrants and pushing their way into the apartment. You'd think they would be discreet and do a sting operation to capture a world-class killer, but the kerfuffle tips her off, leaving Fabolous to find the bathtub empty except for a single red rose and the door to the balcony left open.

The video is wholly absurd from start to finish. For a song so richly colored by descriptions of luxury items and people, the video is shot in black and white to add drama. The plot and styling are presumably an homage to the narrative music videos of earlier decades in hip-hop, but the attempt at film noir, complete with opening credits and a femme fatale, is flimsy when it isn't downright silly. There is a scene where Amber's negligee appears red on-screen in contrast to the black and white. It is supposed to be sexy, but it looks like those sepia-toned photos you see on greeting cards, or framed in your aunt's downstairs bathroom, with little kids dressed in oversized old-fashioned clothing and a boy giving a girl a red rose or a paper heart. Amber inexplicably wears a fur coat throughout an entire dinner date, which is frankly just not that slick. Fabolous cannot lip-synch to save his life. And in the final scene, when Amber escapes, you have to wonder how far she got without someone calling the cops on the woman wearing only a bath towel running for her life. And while I'm overthinking it, what kind of deranged architect puts the balcony off the bathroom?

These overthought thoughts did not cross my mind when I first watched the video from the stage, nor when I watched the handful of other music videos in which Amber appears. When she is on-screen, there is only transfixed

attention and giddy celebration. Amber Rose is more than an
unofficial mascot for strippers, she is our patron saint. Her
rise to mainstream visibility was a testament to the fact that
there was life on the other side of the club that would require
neither repentance nor denial. And what a life it was! People
think that strippers look up to Amber because she got famous
for no other reason than that she was dating Kanye West.
That isn't the reason she's famous, and it isn't the reason we
love her. Amber was already making a name for herself as a
model and video star before Kanye came along. As for dating
Kanye, I could walk into any strip club in Manhattan, throw
a handful of quarters, and hit four strippers who have dated a
famous man at some point. (But I wouldn't do that, because
it is rude and there's nowhere to store change on stripper
apparel.)

There are plenty of famous women to admire besides
Amber Rose who similarly found their way to the top on
the arms of famous men. There are also plenty of famous
women who publicly acknowledge that they were strippers.
Most famous ex-strippers tell tales of redemption from these
sordid ways. More gratingly, several claim they were *no good
at it*, which is really just code for "too good for it." (I see
you, Diablo Cody.) But Amber carried this piece of her past
into the spotlight with her and treated it like the asset it was
instead of the albatross everyone expected. "All the girls were
really cool...I was young, beautiful, I was onstage, I wasn't
really ashamed of my body. I made lifelong friends," she told
Cosmopolitan in 2015.[1]

Though the media treated Amber like an art project that Kanye West pulled from his own imagination and sculpted in bronze and neon, Amber was not a stripper in distress awaiting his rescue. She reportedly stripped until she was twenty-five, with modeling jobs and her first music video cameo coming that same year: "What Them Girls Like" by Ludacris. Transitioning from the club to a successful career outside the adult industry is a testament to the transferable skills learned as a stripper. There is wisdom and art in harnessing one's own desirability and fitting it into the spaces required by the typical strip club patron and then taking them elsewhere as needed. Amber's success became the bridge between the lived reality of being a stripper and being the one-dimensional fantasies strippers are asked to play, with and without their consent.

Among the most important contributions Amber made to dismantling these fantasies was openly discussing that she was in relationships with women for years before dating Kanye.[2] Her bisexuality poured cold water on the myth that strippers are all dick-crazed banshees who see the money as a mere bonus. Amber also changed the tradition of audiences' not often hearing from music video models outside the brief period around the premiere when they are trotted out before the press to discuss what an *honor* it was to work with a *real* artist. But Amber's presence in videos often eclipsed the star power of the artists therein. Strippers who have so often played the animated backdrops and occasional slow-motion booty shots in music videos got a vicarious moment in the sun when the focus was on Amber. Meticulously crafting an image that subverts expectations about women with certain pasts, Amber outstayed the welcome generally extended to such performers and established her own place in the entertainment industry. And though she and Kanye as a couple would be together only two years, Amber stayed on the radar through product endorsements and fashion campaigns, an Instagram of otherworldly sex appeal, a self-help book, and what looks like a genuinely great fucking time.

A radio appearance by Kanye West in early 2015 is instructive of how successfully Amber took ownership of her own image after the breakup. West claimed that he needed to take "thirty showers" after dating Amber before getting with Kim Kardashian in remarks about a recent spat between Khloe Kardashian and Amber on Twitter. More than anything, the remark shows that Amber is impossible to diss artfully. West is arguably the greatest hip-hop wordsmith of his generation, yet he was reduced to making frat-house jabs at Amber for a job she had years ago that she is not ashamed of. A predictable public pile-on soon followed and included her own ex-husband, Wiz Khalifa, briefly adding and later retracting his claims that Amber was an unfit mother by virtue of her past.

Amber responded by arranging a SlutWalk, one of a series of protests designed in response to a rape culture that lays blame on women for their own assaults and for gendered mistreatment more generally. Though SlutWalks have been critiqued for their inadvertent exclusion of marginalized women who experience sexual violence more often and in different ways than the women who started them, Amber's had a distinctly more inclusive feel for which she was commended. In one of the most commonly circulated images from the event, Amber holds up a protest sign that reads "Strippers have feelings too." It is a simple message that appears intended to be funny on its surface. But I read in it a radical statement about the women employed throughout the adult industry onto whom customers project so many fantasies and then demand impatiently that those fantasies be reflected back. I read in it a demand to hear the real women onto whom social anxieties about the nexus where money and gender and sex meet are projected relentlessly but who are not granted permission to voice their own. It is the audacious claim that we are more than the echo chambers for imaginaries of womanhood. And it is a promise that if we didn't want to, we wouldn't have to do a happy little dance on their behalf forever.

All the Lives I Want

Recovering Sylvia

JUST DON'T END UP DOING a Sylvia Plath thing" is not advice that is given to save lives. It is advice given to save face. It is not a warning against the pitfalls of a rotten marriage or the disappointment of publishing only a single novel. It is not intended to help anyone prevent isolation or despair. It is certainly not a thing people say to stop you from sticking your head in the back of an oven. No. Telling people not to do as Sylvia Plath did is universally understood as a good-natured suggestion that a writer not put too much of herself into her creations—lest she accidentally write about something as ordinary as being a woman. For feelings remain the burden and embarrassment of girls. They are not the stuff of art.

Sylvia has become the most recognizable stand-in for the tedious, ill-advised twentieth-century confessional author. Despite her coming of age among a cohort of men describing their own venereal disease as if the pustules themselves were matters worthy of the canon, it is Sylvia's interior life that is so often pointed to as a case of something crass and self-indulgent. To this day, even as Sylvia is long dead by her own hand, her cautionary tale is not about lives poorly lived but about feelings too earnestly expressed. Nearly half a century after her death, we remain more interested in girls' being kept palatable than being kept alive.

The number of hands that have been wrung and fingers that have been wagged at girls who dare to give voice and name to their interior lives suggests that the written history of the world is absolutely awash in the stuff. But the female voice, and the girl's voice especially, is characterized mostly by the deafening silence it emits from the canon. To read the historical record without context suggests that female self-awareness was a genetic anomaly that emerged in the eighteenth century and remained exceedingly rare until the second half of the twentieth century. Those who dare to document their lived experience as worthwhile are brave new girls indeed. As brightly as these girls shine, there remain wet blankets around every corner attempting to extinguish the flames in their hearts. They are dismissed as excessively feminine and juvenile, two words that mean the same thing in the hearts and minds of critics who would sooner praise a six-volume gaze at a Norwegian man's navel than consider the possibility that there are treasures in the hearts of girls. There is no girl that such critics have tried to extinguish more diligently than young Sylvia herself. In the years following her death, she has been accused of culpability in suicides that took place fifty years after her own, along with single-handedly ushering in the idea of suicide as glamorous by people who have apparently never heard of Ernest Hemingway or Jesus Christ. The fact of the matter remains that young women are easy to destroy and doubly easy to destroy if they are already dead. Fortunately, it is also historically the habit of young girls to practice witchcraft, and so the girls keep bringing Sylvia back to life.

Young girls are smarter than they're given credit for, and more resilient, too. They like what they like for good reason. They seek to build kingdoms out of their favorite people and things, and there is a certain subset of girls, even today, who have made Sylvia their icon-elect. The reputation of young girls for "wearing their hearts on their sleeves" is one that is discussed more often as unwittingly sharing too much information, rather than framing them as active agents making decisions on how best to publicly express themselves. Public derision is directed at girls wearing T-shirts of boy bands or one half of a best-friend-necklace pairing because we assume that such unsubtle devotion is the result of juvenile obliviousness, rather than bold and certain admiration. There is intention behind both the words and the images these girls share in their modes of self-expression, intention that we overlook at the peril of our own understanding of how affections operate throughout a lifetime.

At the convergence of adolescent admiration for Sylvia and the penchant to wear one's interests in literal and visible

ways is a massive selection of Sylvia paraphernalia available
for purchase online. I discovered this treasure trove by
accident when looking for a canvas bag with a quote from
Joan Didion on the online crafting marketplace Etsy. I found
the bag in an online shop that featured loads of items inspired
by Sylvia Plath's words and face. I conducted a search for her
name that rendered 399 results. In contrast, "Joan Didion"
presented a single page of 11 crafts dedicated to the author.
A search for Flannery O'Connor and all of her haunted glory
netted 35 results. The closest iconic twentieth-century author
I could search, Toni Morrison, trailed with 58 items.

The clothes featuring Sylvia's image and words vary
wildly in cost and quality, but they are a collection so diverse
in color, design, and selected imagery and text that one could
wear nothing but Sylvia-related garments for weeks before
anyone detected the pattern. In my initial search in the late
fall of 2015, I discovered a pair of flats featuring her portrait,
some poetry, and an image of her tombstone.[1] And then
there are the necklaces. Oh praise God, the *necklaces*! There
are brass lockets on long chains and short typed quotes in
literary serif fonts protected by a layer of glass, and there are
small portraits of Sylvia in the style of a cameo. I imagine
these pieces strewn across young necks throughout the world,
standalone best-friend necklaces for the kind of girl who
prefers the company of ghosts.

Beyond clothing and accessories, one could build a whole
aesthetic around Sylvia trinkets, and I'm sure there are girls

who have. Their bodies and pencil cases are transformed to shrines for the poet whose words helped them exhale at last what it meant to feel in the world as a girl. There is even a criminally unrepresentative doll meant to be Sylvia.[2] It would be nice to believe that the women who make and purchase these devotional items are simply unaware of the disdain Sylvia has incurred from the literary establishment, but as a mere matter of probability, I have my doubts that they are.

"Sylvia Plath's remarkable position today is only partly due to the brilliance of her writing" is as dull a way to start a book as it is an obvious one, but it is how Marianne Egeland begins *Claiming Sylvia Plath: The Poet as Exemplary Figure.* Of course a beautiful, brilliant, mentally tortured, and dead young woman is going to be made something more special in the public imagination than a plain and neurotypical one who succumbs to heart failure in old age. Though Egeland admits in her final chapter that this mythology is more about how Sylvia has been used than how she herself lived or created, the narration at times makes Sylvia's actions appear as if they were intended to be the spark to light some greater movement. "Killing herself in the same year that *The Feminine Mystique* (1963) was published by Betty Friedan, and leaving behind two small children and a manuscript of outstanding poems, Plath seemed to confirm romantic notions about the poet and to demonstrate the difficulties women artists had of surviving in a man's world," she writes.[3] In other words, it was stunt marketing by asphyxiation.

In the *New York Review of Books*, Terry Castle goes so far as to blame Sylvia for the suicide of her son Nicholas in Alaska forty-six years after her own death. The facts that Alaska has the second-highest rate of suicide of any US state and that mental illness is widely accepted as genetic were immaterial, apparently, in the face of an opportunity to use the turn of phrase "Lady Lazarus caught up with him at last." It is clever and spooky indeed, but it is hardly fair. That Castle uses the same piece to accuse Sylvia of making "a sensation still (sometimes) among bulimic female undergraduates" is but one of the scores of dismissals of life-threatening illness among young women as frivolous lifestyle habits.[4]

I was such an undergraduate, unknowingly worshipping at the altar of Sylvia before I formed the bridge in my mind from her work to her face and legacy. I regret not having been one of her apostles as a girl, but I am glad to have found her when I did: in my late twenties and on a mission of almost evangelical zeal to make the emotions of young women not just visible in the literary world but to make them essential components of it. Sylvia's work had lingered in my periphery as it did for many girls who had not been assigned *The Bell Jar* in school but who managed to find her image sprinkled across the sadder corner of the women's Internet.

I began frequenting anorexia and bulimia blogs in the late 1990s in the hopes of catching one of the few diseases that people actively covet. In an age before ubiquitous digital photography, these online shrines to eating disorders were home to meticulously curated collections of images scanned from magazines alongside quotes that ennobled the disease with a sense of almost divine purpose. A quote from Sylvia's poem "In Plaster" made frequent appearances. "She doesn't need food, she is one of the real saints," it read, ripped brutally from its context in a poem about battling a personified disorder but ultimately starving the sickness to its own death. One of the most famous images of Sylvia served as the avatar for many users of the blogging platform LiveJournal, which I followed in the early 2000s, along with images of Twiggy and Brigitte Bardot.

I am glad that I found Sylvia by accidentally falling down a hole of her words alone, unstrangled by their troubling literary legacy. I was searching for a clever turn of phrase I knew was hers to quote to a man when I was twenty-nine years old. I didn't know if it came from a novel or from her diaries, so I was looking up her quotes on the website Goodreads. The site is a helpful cheat sheet for those of us who appear to have read far more than we have; it features book reviews, quotes, and synopses of books and also serves as an odd consortium of legitimate bibliophiles and bizarrely resentful readers alike. Somehow I missed *The Bell Jar* in my formal education but saw it on enough bookshelves at friends' homes to intuit that it was something I needed to eventually find time for on an extracurricular basis.

But where even prolific authors sometimes have a dozen or so web pages filled with quotes, Sylvia had over thirty.

This would be unremarkable but for the fact that she wrote only one novel and a handful of poetry collections. This is a function of the site's more democratic tools: Users can submit quotes and vote on them so that they are arranged in order of their popularity. Just as her Etsy story confirmed, for a sad woman dead quite young, she had certainly made an impression. With more than ten thousand votes, the quote at the very top had nearly double the votes of those of the two runners-up that dwindled in the range of five thousand or so. It read:

> I can never read all the books I want; I can never be
> all the people I want and live all the lives I want. I can
> never train myself in all the skills I want. And why do
> I want? I want to live and feel all the shades, tones and
> variations of mental and physical experience possible
> in my life. And I am horribly limited.

I found myself unmoved by the sentiment and reluctantly disappointed in the readers who had flocked to the site to vote it into the top spot. I had such high hopes for these devoted girls. Sure, I, too, have been frustrated by my own finitude at times. I have mourned the doctor and the movie star and the teenage witch I never became. I can't speak any foreign languages as well as I'd like to, nor can I juggle or play the piano. But when it comes to living and feeling all the shades of life, I have had quite enough of the ups and downs of mood and tone and would be perfectly content for dull tranquility to replace the sound and speed of chaos. Sylvia and I were off on the wrong foot.

Holding the honor of second place was the quote "If you expect nothing from somebody you are never disappointed." This had always been something of a personal motto, and so I felt back on track to liking this woman the girls couldn't stop talking about. In third was "Kiss me, and you will see how important I am." This was the kind of thing I wished I had said to a man when I was much younger, had I been in possession of some shred of that conversational boldness. I developed a literary tongue only after such darling proclamations would have long been inappropriate. I immediately bought a necklace bearing the quote from a store on Etsy. I have never worn it, but I have photographed it lying in my palm on more than one occasion.

I finally found the retort I was looking for on the fifth page of quotes. It read "No day is safe from news of you," and it comes from Plath's poem "The Rival." I planned to use it in the event of receiving a text message from a man I'd been dating for five months who had disappeared unceremoniously on Christmas Eve, despite prior plans and his knowing that I would spend my favorite holiday alone were he to cancel. The line was meant to be a clever way of saying that I had been following his social media accounts, knowing full well that despite the existence of the term "ghosting" that we now have for abandoning romantic interests without a word, he was, quite unfortunately, not at all dead. I didn't use it on him when he reemerged, but I was grateful for having made the excursion to the pages and pages of Sylvia quotes. Further excavation brought me a wealth of gems about love and loss and death. They have all the wit of Dorothy Parker and the devastating brutality of Virginia Woolf. Yet somewhere along the line, the literary establishment lost sight of the genius because they saw it as too wrapped up in girlishness, a niche interest that half the world endures.

I fell in love with Sylvia in that scroll of disjointed quotes and fell with an enthusiasm I had not felt since college when I discovered the especially unforgiving love songs of the Magnetic Fields and the renewed rage of a mid-career Fiona Apple. Sylvia's words were reflections on love and doubt and suffering and the brutal nexus where they all come together in a tender corner of the human heart ("You are a dream; I hope I never meet you"). But they were also nonsense and melodrama without their contexts ("I have suffered the atrocity of sunsets"). I went through page after page until the quotes came to an end, and throughout my read, I tried to put together *The Bell Jar* in something like order only to realize it is a chronicle of disorder. When their origins weren't labeled, I wondered which quotes came from her poetry and which from her diaries, trying to detect either her bright-eyed teen years or the shadow-stricken days that drew her toward the light at the back of the oven. I wondered if ovens had lights in the back in 1963.

Her words made me want to see her face, but there was only one image that dominated the Google image search: Plath in a half-grinning portrait in which she seems confidently unimpressed. Her hair hangs just below her shoulders and is pinned on the left side of her head. She's wearing a cardigan of some sort. She looks like she's in possession of either a brand-new secret or a very old one, and it's how I've seen many women writers look at readings when they've been asked asinine questions by men. But knowing this image well, I searched for more images. I turned to Tumblr, where enterprising young people have reliably excavated archives of lesser-known pictures to bring texture and time to the lives of those who are long dead. These young curators did not disappoint.

I found her unflattering school portrait, better left to the dustbin for such a beauty. I found her wearing a white pillbox hat as she gazes at her interview subject, Elizabeth Bowen, during an assignment for *Mademoiselle*. There was an image of her lying on the beach with her eyes closed, bronzed and grinning in a strapless white swimsuit. It seemed Plath was always wearing swimsuits, even in the absence of any evidence of nearby water. In another photo, she wears a modest two-piece swimsuit and holds a dandelion as if it were a pet, the note reading that this was taken in 1954, during her "platinum summer." In another, she wears a black halter top and takes a drink, of what I can only assume is an adult beverage. She appears as mostly an outline blur on the cover of *The Colossus and Other Poems*, bedecked in a scarf or cape of some kind, and she is a smile incarnate on the cover of her unabridged journals. For all the unruliness of her heart, she was certainly a compliant subject for photographers.

I write of these photographs as if I found them in rapid, orderly succession on Tumblr, but anyone familiar with the platform knows that its treasures do not come that way. Instead, these images are tucked into the folds of the infinite scroll that a reader finds when entering "Sylvia Plath" in the search bar. It is overwhelmingly the same quotes from Goodreads given new life in bigger, more artful fonts. I hoped to find rhyme and reason in them, an evident winner like the one on Goodreads: one quote to rule them all. But on Tumblr, each girl who posts about Sylvia Plath has her own kingdom to run. She cannot necessarily be bothered with choosiness. But when she can be bothered to choose, she will be meticulous to the point of obsession about making the correct choice.

Many of the girls I find on Tumblr reblog Plath quotes mechanically alongside a mountain of melancholy content. They are found with photos of wilted flowers and tattoos in Courier New and the occasional textual allusion to glorifying anorexia. These girls create heaping monuments to pain and subsequently gain impressive followings that suggest the world is every bit as heartbroken as we've suspected all along. Others are more careful curators, and they share less often but more thoughtfully. Sylvia quotes appear alongside photos of Virginia Woolf with her own words scrawled over them and GIFs of Fiona Apple writhing uncomfortably in her own sexualized body. The suffering is palpable in these media. Regardless of the format, it bears the fingerprints of femininity thrown off balance. With all that smiling she did in photos, she struck me as the kind of woman who didn't want to cause a lot of trouble except when she was ready to cause nothing short of a disaster.

There are occasional photos of Sylvia's books themselves and even more of books opened to particularly moving passages by her, a post habit to which I myself must also confess when I cannot resist transmitting a cutting word from Simone Weil or Flannery O'Connor or passages from that lonely grouch of a poet, R. S. Thomas, into the digital world. The open books feature in orderly stacks on white backdrops and on dirty sheets. There are also a number of tattoos of quotes from Sylvia's books, her words etched forever onto female skin and preserved, at least for now, on the Internet for the masses to admire, judge, and envy accordingly. There is even an entire Tumblr account devoted to her words on skin, Sylvia Plath Ink.[5] Many of the tattoos featured there are still surrounded by inflamed skin, indicating that these were photographed as brand-new markings and that their owners urgently wished to share with the world how their bodies and her words had become one.

"I desire the things that will destroy me in the end," a collarbone reads. A rib cage cries out, "I am terrified by this dark thing that sleeps in me," alongside a flower. I find a thigh bearing the words:

The claw
Of the magnolia
Drunk on its own secrets
Asks nothing of life.

Like the T-shirts on Etsy, the tattoo designs are impressively diverse in their colors and placements and the substance of their messages. But I find myself returning over and over to an image of skin bearing the haunting finale of *The Bell Jar*: "I am, I am, I am." Sometimes it is unpunctuated. Sometimes it is etched next to an ideographic heart, and other times it is etched onto a realistic rendering of the heart as human organ. Sometimes it is accompanied by its preceding line, "I took a deep breath and listened to the old brag of my heart." I struggle to think of any line of thinking more linked to being a socialized female than to consider the declaration of simply existing to feel like a form of bragging. But that, of course, is the plight of the feeling girl: to be told again and again that her very existence is something not worth declaring.

To read Sylvia's diaries is to bear witness to an urgent catastrophe. Though the entries are not marked with dates, it quickly becomes clear that the days she chronicles are eventful only insofar as her feelings are events themselves. And that they are. New boys have approximately the same weight as the whole wide world, yet they have taken the liberty of taking up much more than their physically allotted spaces with larger gestures and excessive speech. They suffocate girls' spaces, their intrusions of volume and flesh lingering long after they've left. "In the air was the strong smell of masculinity which creates the ideal medium for me to exist in," she confesses, a rare and raw admission of how much we sometimes crave the opportunity to crawl into the arms of men who cannot or choose not to love us as fully as we do them. Sylvia describes the fickle affections of men in her early years in one-dimensional terms, speaking in the absolutist language that would come to characterize her observations of life in early adulthood. She writes, "Being born a woman is my awful tragedy. From the moment I was conceived I was doomed to sprout breasts and ovaries rather than penis and scrotum; to have my whole circle of action, thought and feeling rigidly circumscribed by my inescapable femininity." Sylvia does not have just best friends, she has the *absolute best friends that history has ever produced.* "She is something vital," she writes of a dear friend, imbuing the girl not just with significance in her life but with life-giving properties no less critical than the beat of a heart or the shine of the sun. Her experience of love has similarly high stakes. "What did my fingers do before they held him? What did my heart do, with its love?" Plath experiences first love as a reincarnation, unable to remember a time when her body had any purpose but the love before her. These are not expressions of hyperbole so much as they are expressions of gravity. These diaries are an exercise in the belief that the ordinary female life is no ordinary thing at all.

When she considers what it means to be a young woman,

she feels the full weight of both its peculiar fragility and its attendant lack of mercies. Sylvia knows full well that the world had neither her particular intellect nor her body in mind when it was designed. At eighteen, she berates herself for the urge to gaze inward, but she cannot find a reprieve from her own fascination:

> I am a victim of introspection. If I have not the power to put myself in the place of other people, but must be continually burrowing inward, I shall never be the magnanimous creative person I wish to be. Yet I am hypnotized by the workings of the individual, alone, and am continually using myself as a specimen.

Sylvia was an early literary manifestation of a young woman who takes endless selfies and posts them with vicious captions calling herself fat and ugly. She is at once her own documentarian and the reflexive voice that says she is unworthy of documentation. She sends her image into the world to be seen, discussed, and devoured, proclaiming that the ordinariness or ugliness of her existence does not remove her right to have it. You might be so very good and generous if you could only relinquish that nagging sense that you matter at all, the world tells them now and told Sylvia then. The ongoing act of self-documentation in a world that punishes female experience (that doesn't aspire to maleness) is a radical declaration that women are within our rights to contribute to the story of what it means to be a human. I look to the girls and women who adore Sylvia on Tumblr and mourn that I had no such home for self-expression and mourn for a world that won't allow itself to behold the richness of their lives as the art of ingénues rather than the nuisances of adolescence.

Clicking through the profiles of girls who share Sylvia-related images and words, it is not uncommon to find images of self-inflicted wounds displayed through carefully selected filters. Reds are turned up and backgrounds are darkened. There is a young Parisian whose scroll is a well-curated collection of literary quotations relating to the discomfort of being human. Another describes herself as having a "rebel soul and a whole lot of gypsy," her account a gallery celebrating literature and landscapes meant to break the heart. These young women awaken a maternal impulse in me, and at some points I get close to reaching out to encourage them to get care. I realize this is both invasive and unproductive at first, but I later realize that it is an underestimation of their capabilities. The very act of sharing the images is a way of seeking care, not as cries for help or as declarations of their suffering. Their blood is proof that something is alive in them. They are making art of their pain. Many experience these platforms as communities where their pain is acknowledged in gentle, more reassuring ways than those available from family and in-person peers.

"Now I know what loneliness is, I think. Momentary loneliness, anyway. It comes from a vague core of the self—like a disease of the blood, dispersed throughout the body so that one cannot locate the matrix, the spot of contagion," Sylvia wrote. I wish I could tell them to stop hurting themselves and have them miraculously listen. I also want to tell them that I am so happy they've found one another instead of finding the back of an oven. I want to tell them that the contagion source is not dispersed in the blood but in fissures in the heart. These fissures do not course through the body and require an aggressive medicinal annihilation. They require the tender touch of one willing to deal with the brokenness of the flesh, and they require the trust of the wounded heart's owner to know that their insides can and should be beheld.

I want to call out to the girls who repeat Sylvia's poisonous directive, "I must bridge the gap between adolescent glitter and mature glow." This is a fallacy, a lie intended to kill the spirits of girls so that they might become what we have come to expect of women. It is telling that among the ranks of quotes on Goodreads and in the bottomless scrolls on Tumblr, it is words from Sylvia's earlier works in her late teens and early twenties that are the most popular. The girls may repeat her longing to grow from glitter to glow, but their affections favor glitter overwhelmingly. Glitter is the unbridled multitudes of shining objects that have no predictable trajectory and no particular use but their own splendor. A glow is contained. Its purpose is to offer a light bright enough that those who bear it will cast a shadow, but not so bright that their features will come fully into focus. "Never surrender your glitter" sounds like the cliché battle cry of a cheerleading coach or a pageant mom, but I still find it a suitable message for young girls.

I also want to show them a line of Sylvia's poem "Stings," written from the point of view of a bee:

> *They thought death was worth it, but I*
> *Have a self to recover, a queen.*

In the end, it was Sylvia who thought that death was worth it indeed, but her disciples now can and should have the chance to feel like queens. The thing about that beloved quote I was so originally unimpressed by, about all the lives Sylvia wanted, is that it continues into a more tender consideration of what it means to be fully who we are. She acknowledges that though she is limited, she is not incapacitated or wounded. She writes, "I have much to live for, yet unaccountably I am sick and sad. Perhaps you could trace my feeling back to my distaste at having to choose between alternatives. Perhaps that's why I want to be everyone—so no one can blame me for being I."

The girls who adorn their persons and bedrooms and websites with the work of Sylvia Plath, who allow her words and images and sounds to give shape to their lives, are her legacy. Defying the command that they not end up like Sylvia, they document their lives in details that are always personal, and they do so in kingdoms they've crafted and breathed meaning into themselves. The ways they tag and arrange their posts are signals in the night, reaching out to others enduring suffering and nonsense in a world that tells them their hearts are burdens rather than treasures. They are good witches in the wilderness and sages and romantics regardless of any present romance. And they know they are not drawn to the bulb at the back of the oven, but by the flare signals sent out by their fellow travelers. They are flashes of light and recognition, momentary reflections of the sun onto a shred of glitter. But they are something vital nonetheless.

Heavenly Creatures

The Gospels According to Lana, Fiona, and Dolly

This is what makes us girls,
We all look for heaven and we put our love first.
　　　—Lana Del Rey, "This Is What Makes Us Girls"

F IONA APPLE WAS BORN FIONA Apple McAfee-Maggart, the child of an actor father and a singer mother. Her birth name was a mouthful for a performer whose record label wanted to package her as something more ethereal. But the clumsiness of her full name is at home in a childhood spent volleying between Los Angeles summers with her father and school years with her mother in an eclectic New York apartment that featured, among other bizarre decorative flourishes, a crucified Kermit the Frog stuffed animal on the kitchen wall. Fiona's team reportedly considered endless variations of her names when they were crafting an image for her that they could sell. Fiona's only reported request was to not include "Apple" in the name. She told *Rolling Stone* in 1998 that in the end, her contract arrived and her stage name was unceremoniously declared "Fiona Apple" before she was able to object. She said the metaphor didn't strike her immediately: "The apple: the thing that starts all the knowledge, but that also starts all the trouble."[1]

Lana Del Rey came into the world as Elizabeth Woolridge Grant, the child of two Manhattan advertising executives who retreated to the more tranquil boredom of Lake Placid, New York, when she was an infant. It is a digestible, Waspy name certainly, though the wealth and nobility of her background have been in constant dispute since her detractors came for blood in the wake of discovering she had not sprung into the world as a devastated femme fatale. Like much of her life and legend, the origins of Lana's stage name are shrouded in mystery. Her name's *meanings* are more easily discoverable. "Lana" is the Gaelic for "child," while "Del Rey" is Spanish for "of the king." This combination is ripe with possibilities for interpretation. The girl child of a king is most literally a princess. More critically, the king can refer to Christ or God himself, his child being either a protégé or a disciple. In any of these cases, where she comes from is explicitly a place of male power. She languishes and thrives under it in due course, but never escapes from that inheritance.

Both women are preternaturally beautiful in that way that makes them hard to look at for too long. Their beauty gives you the sense that it might break something, if it hasn't already. But in appearance, they share little more than alluring looks and occasionally similar tawny waves of hair—when Lana is not indulging her predilection for more dramatic colors. Fiona Apple's center of gravity is her eyes; Del Rey's is her mouth. A Quietus story on Lana from 2011 called her figure "hardy" and "healthy,"[2] which stands in stark contrast to the endless speculations that littered media coverage around the time of Fiona's debut that she was in imminent danger of dying because of her low weight. The press obsessively remarked on Fiona's slight frame, calling her anorexic as an accusation more than a diagnosis.

Both women draw apt comparisons to their husky, soulful counterparts from yesteryear. Lyrically, they both toil endlessly under the gazes of a sordid assortment of men. They know too well the violent hypnosis of those who hope to possess them—men who can smell the blood on the places where a woman is breaking. And Fiona and Lana have wounds to spare. But what sets them apart further from many of their musical peers are their preoccupations with the theological: the question of how God is present and active (or absent) in their lives. In both of these fragile but well-constructed worlds, the ultimate manifestation of the male gaze is to be witnessed by God. But they diverge sharply when it comes to what that gaze means and how they might be rescued from it or, in some cases, redeemed by it.

"Who is that girl? She's going to die soon," my friend Andrea's grandmother asked, going from one thought to the next about Fiona Apple before either of us had time to respond.

It was the summer of 1997, and we were watching the video for "Criminal," the instantly infamous piece of music video history wherein the teenage Fiona appears in her underwear alongside a number of faceless, similarly famished youths. People could not decide if the video was more outrageous because it was a glorification of child pornography or a glorification of anorexia. In either case, blame was hurled at Fiona herself rather than on the much older music executives who were largely responsible for establishing her brand.

From a marketing standpoint, they made an excellent choice. The perverse brand that rendered the teen Fiona the commissioner of her own exploitation was one that girls of a certain age and disposition were enthralled by. We were the kind of girls who fantasized about looking beautiful at our funerals instead of our weddings. But we were not girls who especially wanted to die. In Fiona we sensed a similar disconnect, a fascination with death that did not translate to finding a sense of solace in its promises. I was too young to imagine Fiona as a friend, so I thought of her as an older sister. Her particular neuroses and heartbrokenness were far enough away from my reality to make them romantic in a way that the very real afflictions of my own households were not. Like Fiona, Lana let death linger in her mind long enough for her to breathe it out of her mouth and let it seep out into the world like smoke, the poison all the more appealing when it was mixed with her overtures on love.

Years after taking my posters of Fiona looking character-istically forlorn off my walls and removing her music from heavy rotation on my playlists, I am still touched from time to time by hearing news of Fiona that indicates something like healing in her life. Even as her music matured into something too sophisticated for my untrained ears and my overactive heart, I consumed stories about her like a consummate fan. Whereas the happiness of former idols like Billy Corgan of the Smashing Pumpkins has made me lose interest, I remain invested in Fiona as a person. I wanted her to win, at what game, I am unsure. I did not feel this protective of a female musician again until I was over twenty-five years old, well past the age Fiona was when I drifted from her music.

In February 2011, Lana Del Rey tweeted, "Reputation is what men and women think of us; character is what God and angels know of us." It is a clever take on the concepts of perception and persona, but it is not hers. The quote comes from the eighteenth-century political theorist Thomas Paine, though Lana did not mention this in the tweet. She was a new face on the music scene, four months away from releasing her self-directed music video debut of the song "Video Games." The video made her an indie darling for a few fleeting months before it became the primary piece of evidence used against her when information and images surfaced online about Lizzy Grant: a cute, blond, and far less alluring pop singer than Lana. Whoever managed her marketing efforts had effectively killed Lizzy Grant and replaced her with the pouting temptress Lana Del Rey. Audiences felt duped and sought to punish her for their own suspensions of disbelief.

Lana would soon be accused of performing as a false

persona that was too meticulously manufactured. Rather than an image that was especially dangerous, as people claimed Fiona's had been, Lana's was derided for being artificial and self-indulgent. Lana's femme fatale looks and her hypernostalgic music videos looked labored and amateurish, how a high school girl who got her hands on some old Hollywood movies and a bustier might adorn herself more than how an adult artist with a legitimate interest in a genre might. Fiona was accused of glamorizing child porn in the Hollywood Hills; Lana was accused of pornifying authentic Hollywood glamour.

Those who accuse these women of fraud in their image craft seem not to have heard of David Bowie's successful alter ego Ziggy Stardust or even Bob Dylan, the folksy creation of a genius named Robert Allen Zimmerman. There is a tradition of male artists taking on personae that are understood to be part of their art. It is as though there is so much genius within them that it must be split between these mortal men and the characters they create. Women who venture to do the same are ridiculed as fakers and try-hards; their constructed identities are seen as attention-seeking stunts more than new embodiments of the artists themselves. Madonna is perhaps the most successful woman to reinvent herself but never to fully slip into an alter ego, and even she is routinely called an insufferable bitch for it.

But within what is meant to be the exclusive territory of men who invent and inhabit images that add up to more than the sum of their aesthetic and musical parts, there is a trespasser. She has gone undetected for decades, despite having crafted a highly visible and truly magnetic image. Like Lana and Fiona, she is powerfully moved by the wiles of careless men but is motivated, too, by the surveillance of God, who seems to care even as he judges her. That artist is Dolly Parton, a performer so rigorously committed to her craft that she has not publicly broken character once in a career spanning more than forty years. Famously taking her image cues from "the town tramp" of her rural Appalachian origins, Dolly can reliably be found in a wardrobe of formfitting dazzlers that accentuate her large bust and tiny waist and are always topped off with a blond hairdo that is as much a production as her stage shows. The visual of Dolly's full face of bright makeup, even brighter jewel-toned outfits, and bleached hair appears in sharp contrast to the subdued auburns, deep reds, and earthen tones of Lana and Fiona, of course. But beneath these exteriors are hearts breaking under the cold oscillation between negligence and affection of those whose love they seek.

Fiona's first hit, "Criminal," centered on confession: "I've been a bad, bad girl / I've been careless / With a delicate man." She reportedly wrote the song in under an hour when she was seventeen years old. Record executives listened to the album in progress that would become *Tidal* and said she did not have any hits. And so, on command, she wrote them a hit. There is something perverse about a child writing a song implicating herself in the decline of a man, like the abused Dolores discovering that she had been Lolita all along, inadvertently hurting Humbert Humbert. Fiona declares early in the song, "And I need to be redeemed / To the one I've sinned against / Because he's all I ever knew of love." These lines could be read as a deification of the delicate man of whom she spoke earlier, but the lines "I've done wrong and I want to suffer for my sins / I've come to you 'cause I need guidance to be true" negate such a premise quickly with the hints of godly intercession. Fiona seeks redemption for her sins, unaware that she is not nearly so guilty as she feels. Lana, in sharp contrast, courts sin actively.

Lana's first hit, "Video Games," centered on seduction: "I heard that you like the bad girls / Honey, is that true?" Unlike Fiona, she is not a girl recognizing her own sin in penitential retrospect; she is a woman broadcasting it, perhaps exaggerating the authenticity of her own wickedness as sex appeal. Lana surrenders to man rather than God, begging to retreat to the shadows of the narcissistic but ordinary men whose toxicity seems to intoxicate her. "It's you, it's you, it's all for you / Everything I do / I tell you all the time / Heaven is a place on earth with you / Tell me all the things you want to do," she sings. Her cry is desperate and real; you believe her when she says it is all for him, her passion momentarily letting her audience forget that this complete devotion to a man whose company she considers akin to that of God and the company of heaven is playing video games, of all the mundane activities in the world.

In the video-cum-short-film *Tropico*, Lana appears as

both Eve in the Garden of Eden and as a retro 1970s version of the Virgin Mary in the first portion of the film, which is set to the song "Body Electric." Before an audience of Elvis Presley, Marilyn Monroe, and Jesus Christ himself, she dances seductively with Adam before biting into the forbidden fruit and suddenly losing her footing. She falls not onto soil but onto the stage of a strip club, now wearing lingerie with a flutter of bills falling around her as "Gods and Monsters" begins. "God's dead, I said 'Baby, that's alright with me,'" she declares, not so much an atheist as an apostate. Lana does not even make an effort to couch her rejection of God in euphemisms as she declares, "Me and God, we don't get along, so now I sing." She adds insult to injury when she sings, "In the land of Gods and Monsters / I was an Angel / Looking to get fucked hard." The rejection of God is not enough for Lana; she must also replace him with a man, the less holy the better.

Before the world was treated to the harshness of Fiona's self-flagellation or the defiance of Lana's sexuality, Dolly gave us her first hit in "Just Because I'm a Woman," a song centered on forgiveness. "Now a man will take a good girl / And he'll ruin her reputation / But when he wants to marry / Well, that's a different situation," Dolly sings of the hypocrisy of a man who will ruin a woman's reputation but not marry her, insinuating that premarital sex is the cause for his judgment. "Now I know that I'm no angel / If that's what you thought you'd found / I was just the victim of / A man that let me down," she continues, acknowledging what she sees as the sin of her own actions, but not without holding a man accountable for bringing her to that sin.

The presence of God in Dolly's music is more obvious than in the songs of Lana or Fiona, but hidden under sparkling jumpsuits and bright blush, there is profound theological darkness. Dolly's 1971 hit "Coat of Many Colors" recounts how her impoverished mother sewed rags together to make her a coat, the resulting garment more likely to be a clashing eyesore than Joseph's dazzling robe from the book of Genesis that signaled his father's favor. The young Dolly in the song tries to tell the Bible story to her classmates who ridicule her coat, but it falls on deaf ears among godless children. The narrative of 1971's "Letter to Heaven" seems more at home in Flannery O'Connor's macabre oeuvre than in Dolly's. In the song, a little girl has her grandfather pen a letter to her dead mother, which she intended to be sent skyward toward God's kingdom, only to be struck by a car and killed on her way to the post office to mail it. It closes, "The postman was passing and picked up the note / Addressed to the Master and these words he spoke / Straight up into heaven this letter did go / She's happy up there with her mommy I know." Were it penned by anyone but Dolly Parton, this song would sound like a crude and cruel joke. But in her capable hands and voice, the only cruelty is that of a god who renders our departed beloveds accessible only if we depart ourselves.

But God is not all inscrutability for Dolly. In "He's Alive," she places herself among the witnesses to the crucifixion and recounts her subsequent doubt that he has risen again. But upon seeing the risen Christ, she embraces him in an ecstatic relief. "And as I looked into His eyes / The love was shining out from Him / Like sunlight from the skies / Guilt in my confusion / Disappeared in sweet release / And every fear I ever had / Just melted into peace," she sings. For Dolly, to be looked upon by God is an opportunity for a welcome surrender. The gaze of men, however, is less gentle in her world.

Obscured by her intoxicating good cheer and reputation as a wholesome if sometimes tacky entertainer, Dolly's markedly melancholic view of love is easy to miss. Even within country music's tradition of tragic romances as the only ones worth singing about, her romantic despair is because her lovers are not dying valiantly but vanishing casually. Lovers routinely abandon Dolly, and when they don't, she lives in fear of their doing so, as she famously described in "Jolene." She begs Jolene not to steal her man, in the forgivable delusion that it is women who steal away men rather than men who relinquish themselves readily. "I have cradled your head on my pillow / Quenched your thirst from my sweet loving cup / I have bowed to your needs like a willow / Now you've gone in the prime of our love," she mourns on "Prime of Our Love." One gets the sense that it was not Jolene who was the problem after all. Dolly is hopelessly dependent on love, declaring, "I am only happy when you are by my side / How precious is this love we share / How very precious, sweet and rare," in "Love Is Like a Butterfly." She has only one source of happiness, and among its defining characteristics is its scarcity. "Do you ever wake up lonely in the middle of the night / Because you miss me, do you darling / Oh, and do your memories ever take / You back into another place in time," she asks in "Do I Ever Cross Your Mind," a song that reads like a thinly veiled confession that he is certainly crossing hers in the ways she describes. Dolly's religious piety may be real, but her obsession with finding the approval of men lingers at the border of worship.

Lana, on the other hand, is more single-minded in her devotions. She is the most dangerous kind of blasphemer, not a denier of God but a creator of her own. "When things get bad enough, your only resort is to lie in bed and start praying. I dunno about congregating once a week in a church and all that, but when I heard there is a divine power you can call on, I did. I suppose my approach to religion is like my approach to music—I take what I want and leave the rest," Lana said in an interview.[3] "Take what you want and leave the rest" is a slogan frequently used in Alcoholics Anonymous, alongside its more strict cousin, "Take what you *need* and leave the rest." Lana has mentioned in passing her involvement in 12-step recovery, and as a former member of this group myself, I can attest to the slogan's value in resisting stringent codes that are not conducive to sobriety. I can also attest to how useful it is when eschewing the hard work required of facing the reality that such codes might have some value or purpose. It is also not unlike her old buddy Thomas Paine's remarks in *The Age of Reason*: "I do not believe in the creed professed by the

Jewish church, by the Roman church, by the Greek church, by the Turkish church, by the Protestant church, nor by any church that I know of. My own mind is my own church."

But while Paine's apostasy is one that goes beyond self-reliance into self-worship, Lana does herself no such favors. There is no apparent solace at the altars of the men she worships. There is only more longing. "When I'm down on my knees, you're how I pray," she sings on "Religion," from her album *Honeymoon*.

On Fiona's sophomore album, *When the Pawn...*, she is noticeably less repentant than on her debut. She is hardened by a music industry that very publicly shamed her for having the audacity to speak human truths, and particularly female truths, on public stages. In the first track, "On the Bound," she sings, "You're all I need," and takes a pause before realizing her real need: "and maybe some faith would do me good." But the difference between Lana and Fiona is that Lana long ago determined that her faith was doing her no good. Fiona grasps at it continually, singing on "Paper Bag," "But then the dove of hope began its downward slope / And I believed for a moment that my chances / Were approaching to be grabbed / But as it came down near, so did a weary tear / I thought it was a bird, but it was just a paper bag." All the divine signs turn out to be the detritus of the world, but Fiona grasps onto it in the vain hope that the next might be something holy.

When Fiona can no longer grasp for the signs of God's love, she accepts an alternative role: the role of the martyrs absorbing the sins of others into her flesh. "And I will pretend / That I don't know of your sins / Until you are ready to confess / But all the time, all the time / I'll know, I'll know / And you can use my skin / To bury your secrets in," she sings in "I Know." Even when she is at last confident that she is not the sinner herself, she sees it her bounden duty to take on the sins of other men, internalizing their wickedness as punishment for the sin of loving them.

But Apple's 2005 album, *Extraordinary Machine*, represents a marked shift away from the hold—and zeros in on the destructive men who cannot appreciate her love. "Oh what a cold and common old way to go / I was feeding on the need for you to know me / Devastated at the rate you fell below me / What wasted unconditional love / On somebody who doesn't believe in the stuff / Oh well," she sings on 2005's "Oh Well." She begins to call out men directly for their transgressions against her, for their failures to love her in return. There is still something of the guilt-ridden girl in her self-professed culpability for allowing such men into her life, but there is effort to move away from it. "But I'm not being fair / 'Cause I chose to listen to that filthy mouth," she confesses on "Not About Love," but she makes an effort to turn away from it. "But I'd like to choose right / Take all the things that I've said that he stole / Put 'em in a sack / Swing 'em over my shoulder / Turn on my heels / Step out of this sight / Try to live in a lovelier light." There is an intentional shift in her tone, an ambition to do more than suffer under men's indifference toward her love. It would be seven more years before she released another album.

A 2012 profile of Fiona in *New York* magazine is considered among the best of its kind and so, too, is the album Fiona released that year, *The Idler Wheel Is Wiser Than the Driver of the Screw and Whipping Cords Will Serve You More Than Ropes Will Ever Do*. Dan P. Lee's storytelling and descriptions are artful indeed, but his extraordinary subject does much of the heavy lifting. Her eyes are like "mint chocolate chip when it melts" and she "was odd-looking in the way most beautiful people are as children." She gets his name wrong constantly, calls him at all hours of the night, and speaks of "mirror neurons" and childhood superpowers.[4] But what was more telling than what Fiona actually did during the profile was the fact that she was doing anything at all: Fiona had made herself so scarce in the twenty-first century that even small peeks into her life would have been revelatory. The great feat of Fiona is her disappearance from the public eye, leaving us to wonder often if she found the redemption and love she sought for so long.

Her last album also is one of self-awareness that revealed despair not quite conquered but certainly more contained. "My love wrecked you / You packed to twirl your skirt at the palace / It hurt more than it ought to hurt / I went to work to cultivate a callus / And now I'm hard, too hard to know / I don't cry when I'm sad anymore, no no," she declares in "Left Alone," a tribute to solitude. In the song "Valentine," she reveals, "I'm a tulip in a cup / I stand no chance of growing up / I've made my peace I'm dead I'm done / I watched you live to have my fun." On the page, her words are stripped of the defiant blues she calls on to sing, making it difficult to convey in words here that this is something like triumph in her acknowledgment that she coexists with memories of these men rather than being haunted by them. When she turns away from the men who will not love her, she finally stops speaking of the sin that plagued her earlier music. It is her most successful to date in terms of critical appeal and chart success, and yet I can listen to it only as background noise; the piano and voice remain familiar but are no longer family. She is not the sister I once knew. She is too far from the oddly ecstatic pain of living under the surveillance of man and God. But Lana remains close.

"We both know the history of violence that surrounds you / But I'm not scared, there's nothing to lose now that I've found you," she sings in "Honeymoon." It is a challenge and a capitulation at once. One gets the sense that this is the same man she watched playing video games and to whom she proudly declared her curses to God and at whom all of her sadness is directed across one album every year for four years. "I know what only the girls know / Lies can buy eternity," Lana confesses in "Music to Watch Boys To," the same track on which she declares, "I live to love you." It is hard to tell if this is the lie that is buying her eternity or some other declaration on the track, like that nothing good can stay or that it's all a game to her.

I am perhaps too eager to choose to believe that "I live to love you" is the lie she is using to manipulate the men she once deified. I want to believe that Lana has also escaped the paralyzing gaze of men whose shadows she found warmth inside of, these puny avatars for God who function as deciders of our fate nonetheless. But even if she is momentarily triumphant in lying about her love as a ticket to salvation, it does not stick. "Getting darker and darker / Looking for love / In all the wrong places / Oh my God / In all the wrong places / Oh my God," Lana moans in "The Blackest Day." She cannot help but cry out to him despite the emptiness of his promise and the cruelty of his gaze.

"I have found Lana Del Rey in the same moments that I have found myself the most dysphorically disenchanted with what I can do," my friend Natasha told me after midnight in the early winter. Natasha is a force that men shatter against but that women can fold into like a blanket. Englishness seeps out in her accent and intonations, but her Russian heritage shapes the pure and terrifying wisdom that pours out of her mouth. Her gestures are massive and her body is minuscule, and she is one of several of my friends I'm still shocked occasionally to think have selected me. She is also one of many friends who share my affection for Lana Del Rey. "We like Lana because none of us are exempt from that which we are sold," she said. And despite all the hand-wringing that went into the fallout following Lana Del Rey's revelation as a persona, Lana is not a dangerous product we were sold. She is a reflection of a logical response to our inheritance. We will be surveilled under a masculine gaze whose warmth or coldness toward us will often be largely out of our control, whether we pass them on the street, surrender our names to them in marriage, or pray to them in the blackness of night. We might as well find love among the ones we can see.

Bearing witness to the vulnerability of Lana is what lets me cling to her when I have largely let Fiona go, confident that even if she has not escaped the memories of these men, she is at peace with them. I have a desire to protect and encourage Lana and women like her, those who suffer the cold but won't step out of the shadows of those who keep them from the light. I want them to take a lesson from the playbook of Dolly Parton, the author of one of the greatest love songs of all time, "I Will Always Love You." Many don't realize that Dolly wrote it because it was made most famous by Whitney Houston—happy proof that its tender message and strength are transferable from one woman's love to another's. The song is not about wanting a man to return, but choosing to walk away from one. It is a bittersweet farewell certainly, but it is the resolute decision of the woman singing it. "I hope life treats you kind / And I hope you have all you've dreamed of / And I wish to you, joy and happiness / But above all this, I wish you love," she sings, devoid of the resentment that so often characterizes breakup songs. It is an offering of forgiveness, and it is the act of mortal love that most closely resembles grace.

There Can Be Only One

On Lil' Kim, Nicki Minaj, and the Art of Manufactured Beef

The function, the very serious function of racism, is distraction. It keeps you from doing your work. It keeps you explaining, over and over again, your reason for being.

—Toni Morrison

Perched in a salon chair that she commands like a throne, Lil' Kim sports a heavy side part through expertly straightened hair that falls in a dramatic swoop over her left eye in a look reminiscent of Veronica Lake. She is being fussed over by a hairstylist, and as her interview begins, she puts on a pair of oversized red sunglasses that match the peacoat she wears buttoned all the way up. Keeping an eye on the stylist as the interview proceeds, it becomes clear that she is not actually doing anything substantive with Kim's hair, which is already perfectly in place. But like wearing the sunglasses and coat indoors, the stylist is there for dramatic effect, the kind of decorative embellishment that amplifies the gravitas of a celebrity. The scene would be unremarkable if not for the fact that it takes place not on MTV but on PhatClips,[1] an underground rap show in St. Louis. It is also early 1996, several months before Kim's debut album, *Hard Core*, is set for release and is at the time still titled *Queen Bee*. She is still mostly known in the rap scene as the sole female member of Junior M.A.F.I.A., a rap crew headed by the Notorious B.I.G. But Kim is the kind of woman who dresses for the job she wants, not the job she has. And the title she's after is the undisputed queen of rap.

When she releases *Hard Core* in November of that year, Kim gets the job as album sales hit 78,000 in the first week and go on to double-platinum certification, an unprecedented feat for a female rapper. I was among the younger buyers of the album at the age of eleven. I expressed little more than a giggly appreciation for Kim's raunchy demands for sex, love, power, and merchandise when I played tracks for friends out of the earshot of parents. We doubled over in laughter at the graphic puns and dirty sketches between tracks, but when I listened to it alone, I felt a visceral shift in my posture and attitude. I was acquainted with Third Wave Riot Grrrl bands performing a brand of sex positivism that functioned mostly as a "Fuck you!" to power disparities in gender and sex, but this was something entirely different. Kim was inverting these same structural powers through her rhymes, not with a "Fuck you!" but a "Fuck me... No seriously, come the fuck over here and fuck me."

"It was almost as if Josephine Baker and Al Capone had raised their lovechild in the wild and then unleashed her on the rap world," wrote critic Terry Sawyer of *Hard Core*'s over-the-top imagery that mixes gangster authenticity with expert feminine seduction.[2] Kim drips with diamonds, accessorizes with an Uzi, and commands an army of willing men to pleasure her on demand. "Hip-hop had never seen anything like Brooklynite Kimberly Jones at the time of her solo debut: She single-handedly raised the bar for raunchy lyrics in hip-hop, making male rappers quiver with fear," read the overview of *Hard Core* in 2004's *The New Rolling Stone Album Guide*.[3] *Hard Core* went beyond setting a new standard in lyrical smut; Kim was declaring war on the political and social structures that dominated her world. And she was going to win. "She says she used to be scared of the 'dick,' but 'now I throw lips to tha shit / Handle it like a real bitch.' Punning with extreme wit— as if her life depended on it, Lil' Kim epitomizes 'uncensored speech.' She embodies it in an ultra-erotic militancy that is relentless; and, sex-wise, she is all about revolution," writes Professor Greg Thomas in *Hip-Hop Revolution in the Flesh: Power, Knowledge, and Pleasure in Lil' Kim's Lyricism*.[4]

But the revolutionary genius of a woman is inherently suspicious to mainstream media, and even more so if that woman is young and black. "Lil' Kim is presumed by elite definitions to be only an object of knowledge ('distraction,' 'entertainment'), not a transmitter of knowledge herself,"

Thomas continues.[5] Her detractors sought out ways to dismiss her brilliance as either a counterfeit or an accident. To this day, critics are quick to suggest that Kim would never have had success without the guidance of Christopher Wallace, aka the Notorious B.I.G., aka Big Poppa, and better known to his friends and fans as "Biggie." *Hard Core* is undoubtedly covered in his fingerprints, but he is participating in *her* revolution. When he sings, "He's a slut, he's a ho, he's a freak / Got a different girl every day of the week" on her breakout hit "Crush on You," it is a clever inversion of gender expectations wherein a man's promiscuity is potential cause for his dismissal rather than a vehicle by which to secure his reputation. Though their personal and professional relationship was tenuous at times, Biggie made clear in no uncertain terms that Kim's genius was her own and championed her project until the end.

"Lil' Kim did not make her Hip-Hop entrance as a sexual minority, an exotic, or some disempowered girl in this storied clique of eight men and one woman. She came in lyrically as 'Lieutenant' to their mentor... She came in as alter ego and heir to the throne—with a royal, matrilineal Blues resonance all her own," writes Thomas.[6] Biggie himself knew well how uneasily the head that wears the crown lies, remarking often on the corrupting influence of fame and money and the jealousy attracted by both. The success of *Hard Core* elevated Kim from the token girl in the crew to a hip-hop force in her own right, a status that threatened her once-devoted male fans.

"She represented a very specific male fantasy, she was the 'cool girl' for thugs. She was a rider and down for everything sexually, and you put up with her asserting herself because you knew at the end of it she was stashing guns for you. But once that was no longer her role, rap guys discarded her," Mychal Denzel Smith told me. As she cultivated a persona and evolved her hip-hop style without help from Puffy or Biggie, rap fans and members of the hip-hop press who had once fawned over Kim abandoned her and sought to replace her. And they saw no better replacement than her own longtime friend and colleague, Foxy Brown.

The origin of the now legendary feud between Kim and Foxy is most often traced back to the week after *Hard Core* was released, when Foxy's own debut, *Ill Na Na*, came out. Though they'd appeared on magazine covers together earlier that year, competing on the charts was assumed to take their feud to the next level. It is taken at face value that *of course* two beautiful and talented women releasing albums within a week of each other in the same genre would throw out years of friendship and solidarity in a trifling competition for the top spot. But the tension between Foxy and Kim was a matter primarily of rumors in that first year, rumors largely fueled by members of their rival entourages, Kim's Junior M.A.F.I.A. and Foxy's The Firm, rather than by the two women. "It didn't have to do with Kim and I personally. It was the people around us," Foxy told *Vibe* in 1998.[7] On her second album, 1999's *Chyna Doll*, Foxy all but dedicated her track "My Life" to Kim: "You was my sister, we used to dream together /

How we could make it real big, do our thing together."[8] But the dispute was never healed and escalated into a shoot-out between their entourages at radio station Hot 97 in 2001, for which Kim eventually served time in prison after lying to a federal grand jury about the events.

"Perhaps Foxy Brown and Lil Kim's sexually liberated hip-hop arrival in the mid-'90s had an unintended side effect, creating a cycle where we boost the most seductive women rappers like a push-up bra and then drop them like DMX on that Slingshot ride once they're older and (ir)regular-looking and have run out of Blackberry phones to throw at people," writes John Kennedy at *Vibe* in 2014, making his case that Kim ought to be respected for the elder statesman of rap that she is, the "Air Jordan of women rappers," in his terms.[9] I agree with Kennedy on all but the point that these consequences are ever unintended. The rift between the two never healed, and though Kim went on to more mainstream success than Foxy, with her 2000 album *The Notorious K.I.M.* shipping platinum in its first week, the feud followed her every move. Kim's reputation as a jealous bitch was cemented in both hip-hop and mainstream media ahead of her reputation as a revolutionary emcee.

In 2009, an emerging rapper named Nicki Minaj began making waves for both her brazenly sexual rhymes and her affinity for over-the-top fashions that appeared to draw direct inspiration from Kim. "I did meet her when I was with Lil Wayne during the I AM Music tour. We chopped it up and I gave her props, but we haven't spoken since. I got nothing but love for her, I think she is one of the key players in this female rap thing, so you can not do nothing but salute Kim," Nicki told Necole Bitchie in 2009.[10] But by the following year, the two were embroiled in a game of she-said/she-said, sparring on hip-hop radio, media, and on diss tracks. To read the media surrounding their feud, it is easy to imagine two vicious, petty women fighting over gossip and embarrassing themselves. But the actual documents tell a different story; both women are ferociously smart, endlessly patient in their interviews, and still relentlessly goaded into talking more shit than they seem to want to. In transcripts and recordings of Kim's interviews about their relationship from the first few years of the feud, she acknowledges the feud but is quick to note how excited she was about Nicki when she was on her way up. Similarly, Nicki's interviews regularly feature her candid admission that Kim is among her most prominent influences. The mainstream media, however, never got the memo about Kim.

"Nicki Minaj is the world's biggest female hip-hop star, a top pop star and the first woman to achieve success in both genres," reads a profile of Nicki by Vanessa Grigoriadis for the *New York Times Magazine* in 2015. This failure to mention Kim's trailblazing crossover into pop stardom is just one of many glaring omissions in the piece. " 'Bitch,' in music, used to be an insult, a sneer, and it still can be. But female empowerment is a trend, and the word has been reclaimed— by Minaj, in many a track; by Rihanna, in 'Bitch Better Have My Money'; and triumphantly by Madonna, in her recent track 'Bitch, I'm Madonna,'" she writes, somehow unaware of the track "Queen Bitch" that came out nearly twenty years before. Perhaps more egregious is the assertion that "early in her career, she also adopted Lady Gaga's method of saturating the media with outrageous costumes," as if Kim's iconic pastel wigs and her showstopping MTV Video Music Awards skintight purple jumpsuit and uncovered breast adorned with matching pasty never happened. Nicki is annoyed at the question and dismisses it as "old."[11]

During the interview, Nicki's agitation reaches a breaking point when Grigoriadis asks a series of questions about the men in her life and career who are feuding with one another. It culminates in Grigoriadis asking Nicki if she "thrives on drama." There is a record scratch of silence, which Nicki breaks by saying, "To put down a woman for something that men do, as if they're children and I'm responsible, has nothing to do with you asking stupid questions, because you know that's not just a stupid question. That's a premeditated thing you just did." Nicki says, "Do not speak to me like I'm stupid or beneath you in any way," before asking Grigoriadis to leave.[12]

The interaction is an eerie echo of the annoyance Kim showed when being interviewed for the *Guardian* in 2013. Her interviewer said, "You seem like you're in a positive place right now—so are your beefing days behind you?" Kim grows exasperated and replies, "That's a premature judgment to make, because I've always been a positive person. People say things about me that they don't understand. No disrespect to you, but you really have to look at what you said—'You seem to be in a positive place now.' You don't know me. When have you ever seen me be negative?"[13] Over and over again, Nicki and Kim are asked to go through the rituals of attending awards shows and going on the radio to discuss their art and are asked to discuss each other. These engagements do not unintentionally fuel these feuds; the fuel is their primary purpose.

"There can be only one," the white-dominated mainstream media insist when it comes to female power players, and they double down on this assertion when it comes to black women. The refusal to let these two women, or any two women, coexist as representatives of boldness and brilliance in hip-hop has the more insidious effect of narrowing their cultural influence into hip-hop exclusively. Their inspiration travels much further than that. Christina Aguilera shed much of her pop image in 2002 with *Stripped*, the tour that saw her in provocative black one-pieces reminiscent of Kim's and with a hip-hop sound and attitude not unlike Kim's. Katy Perry spent years sporting well-manicured pastel hair that Kim brought to popularity. The raunchy stage shows of Miley Cyrus are homages to Kim's envelope-pushing performances, and Cyrus even dressed up as Kim at the 1999 VMAs for Halloween in 2013. And I don't care how many people believe she was the heir apparent to Madonna, Lady Gaga would never have wanted a ride on a "disco stick" if Kim hadn't taken one years earlier on "Magic Stick." Because she is more relevant to today's music consumers than Kim, it is Nicki who is most able to publicly push back against the failure of white female artists and the media that pander to them to acknowledge the tremendous cultural influence of black women artists like Kim.

When the MTV Video Music Award nominations were announced in 2015, Nicki took to Twitter to critique the oversaturation of thin white women in pop music, a comment that Taylor Swift took as a personal attack. The ensuing exchange became something of a spectacle, with Taylor eventually apologizing for her reaction to Nicki's comments. Miley Cyrus responded, "What I read sounded very Nicki Minaj, which, if you know Nicki Minaj is not too kind. It's not very polite. I think there's a way you speak to people with openness and love."[14] The one saving grace of the profile that got Nicki so desperately wrong was that it did capture her fearless response to Cyrus. She said, "The fact that you feel upset about me speaking on something that affects black women makes me feel like you have some big balls. You're in videos with black men, and you're bringing out black women on your stages, but you don't want to know how black women feel about something that's so important? . . . If you want to enjoy our culture and our lifestyle, bond with us, dance with us, have fun with us, twerk with us, rap with us, then you should also want to know what affects us, what is bothering us, what we feel is unfair to us. You shouldn't *not* want to know that."[15] Kim may have actually been the first female rapper to successfully take her music mainstream, but Nicki's intrepid journey into calling out the hypocrisy of the white establishment is a remarkable crossover of its own.

What is lost to all of the manufactured squabbling in Kim's career is the fact that christening herself "Queen Bee" in the 1990s was always about dominating men rather than competing with other women. And though many have attempted to crown Nicki the new Queen Bee, she has resisted the title. Nicki has instead aligned herself with another feminine archetype: the Barbie doll. Kim likened herself to Barbie before Nicki when she rhymed, "Black Barbie dressed in Bulgari / I'm trying to leave in someone's Ferrari," in her 2003 song "The Jump Off," but she has expressed far fewer qualms with Nicki's self-anointment with that title than she has with any allusions to the Queen Bee. Just as there is a matrilineal transfer of power in the beehive, however, Barbie's unapologetically pink kingdom is where the imagination and dreams of girls are the rule of law. And both the queen bee role and the legacy of Barbie are that they hold exalted, enviable positions of power and influence. The reality is that in each of their respective realms, they must work tirelessly and often without reward. They endure the oversights and slights to their contributions, perhaps looking forward to the day when they can live out their artistic and personal commitments without being thrown into such pedestrian disputes. These commitments are also crystallized in "The Jump Off" when Kim declares, "Spread love, that's what a real mob do / Keep it gangsta, look out for her people."

Kim and Nicki might never reconcile, and my holding out for them to do so would be more reflective of my hopes than theirs. But there is solace in knowing that the doll armies and beehives they've empowered and the music they've inspired will be their legacies instead of the tedious feud into which they were thrust. Their creative descendants will know them by the revolution in their art and the strength in their love, the kind of inheritance well suited to represent their audacious empires.

The Queen of Hearts

An Alternative Account
of the Life and Crimes
of Courtney Love

COURTNEY LOVE WAS DEFILING A corpse the first time I encountered her. Or so I thought in 1994 when, while sitting in the waiting room of my dentist's office, I opened to the cover story in *People* magazine about the recent suicide of Kurt Cobain, wherein Courtney is noted as "wearing one of her dead husband's trademark cardigan sweaters" in the first sentence. In the weeks following Cobain's suicide, I imagined him committing the act in the now iconic camel cardigan he wore to perform on *MTV: Unplugged*. I got it in my head that Courtney took this specific garment directly from his body to wrap around herself. The story also mentioned how Courtney had taken a lock of Kurt's hair and washed it, so it was not entirely far-fetched in my eight-year-old mind that she had collected both of these souvenirs in one ghastly fell

ALL THE LIVES I WANT

swoop. And because I did not know then that both grief and romantic love can manifest as corporeal craving, I recognized no purpose in these rituals outside of the occult.

The story featured a black-and-white photo of the greenhouse floor where Cobain was found, with part of his right side sticking out in just enough of the frame to plant a nightmare. His now shattered head was mercifully out of the frame, but his foot was in a sneaker that looked like it belonged to a teenager. My mother saw the photo and quickly confiscated the magazine, briefly looking through the pages herself. "That poor baby," she said before putting the magazine back on the rack. I'm still not sure if she was referring to the infant daughter he left behind or to Cobain himself, but I had no doubt that she wasn't talking about Courtney. I would go on to become enamored of Courtney the following summer, but for those few months, in my mind, she was a mad widow disturbing the dead.

I have always bristled at the description of Courtney as "the girl with the most cake." This spoiled, smug little creature was first introduced in Hole's "Doll Parts" on the band's sophomore album *Live Through This* and has reappeared in nearly every profile of Courtney in the decades since the album's 1994 release. Love's signature guttural moan sounds as much like desire as it does pity, and the accompanying image casts her as the impulsive girl child inside a grown woman's body, a physically and emotionally clumsy brute. We are sad to see her suffer but also know that such children have a tendency to be insufferable. However, pegging Courtney as the gluttonous girl on the delicious brink of her own self-destruction is a mistake. And more and more, I am dissatisfied with the prospect of Courtney's legacy being linked to a girl rather than a woman. I am even dissatisfied with the idea that her legacy will be linked to a human at all. Courtney Love, you see, is a witch.

An eighth grader named Meghan introduced me to *Live Through This*, along with a handful of other neighborhood converts, during the summer of 1994. This consortium of girls who felt a little harder than we ought to often lay on Meghan's bed and stared at the pale green plastic stars affixed to her ceiling and listened to the songs on the album out of order. Meghan played the role of DJ, taking requests that our favorite be played next until we had listened to the entire thing. Until I saw the video for "Doll Parts," I thought that Courtney was the crying beauty queen on the album cover. I imagined her waving to an empty dance hall, winning the contest on the technicality of being its only entrant.

Loving Hole as an adolescent girl was an exercise in comically misinterpreting lyrics but still identifying with their particularly female anguish. My friends and I listened to the stories on *Live Through This* as one might listen to a stranger frantically seeking help in a language other than our own. We detected distress but not its source. Hers were stories littered with drugs and shrieking infants and the kind of girls who never stood a chance against ending up in a box by the bed. This was the foreign country of addiction and panicked motherhood and broken hearts. There was an abundance of bodily fluids: talk of milk run dry and girls who piss themselves. It was all germs and embryos. The panicked cries sounded like something that might be waiting to happen to us, or even waiting inside of us already. Those cries broke our hearts—not just for our newly appointed queen but also for our future selves. A world of women's blood and tears was the one we were on the brink of inheriting and would soon have to live through as well.

In light of its other striking visuals of motherhood, death, and addiction, it is easy to miss that *Live Through This* is thick with witches. The music videos for the album's tracks are shot through with the particular sadness of working-class school dances, and Courtney's commitment to dressing like an overripe figurine during that era links the album to macabre children's games and girls who bleed too early. But a witch first appears in the third track, "Plump," when Courtney shrieks, "My baby's in her arms / Crawling up her legs / Like a liar at a witch trial / You look good for your age." On "Softer, Softest," there are two and a half lines sung with uncharacteristic sweetness, "Burn the witch / The witch is dead / Burn the witch," followed by just the briefest pause before screaming, "Just bring me back her head."

Beyond the explicit references to witches, there is a pronounced misanthropy and a notable commitment to the manipulation of others that borders on shape-shifting. Courtney declares, "I'm the one with no soul," in the opening song "Violet," while there is madness born of missing babies on "I Think That I Would Die" (a classic witch-making formula if there ever was one). "Miss World" and "Doll Parts" are both odes to the woman morally disfigured by virtue only of her own wretched thoughts, barely human in their wantonness. If these are unconvincing pieces of evidence of witchcraft enthusiasm, it is nothing more to me than confirmation that Love has done an especially thorough job with her sorcery.

Meghan's cadre of adolescent girls were devoted disciples of the witchy Love, and we were hardly alone in our devotion. Despite the mourning shrouds that covered the landscape of rock criticism in the days and years that followed Kurt's death, the genius of *Live Through This* was not entirely obscured by its attendant tragedies. The *Rolling Stone* review from 1994 is awash in adoring metaphors: "daydream whispers," "crushed-velvet guitar distortion," and "a woman who measured the depth of her abyss by taking the plunge" all feature in David Fricke's praise.[1] The *NME* review concluded, "It wakes rock from its cliché coma, leads it, laughing, to a lake of stinking mud and honey, and there drowns it; quietly, efficiently and with surprising gentleness."[2] *Spin* and *Rolling Stone* both identified it as the best album of 1994. The sheer volume of positive criticisms surrounding the release that were written primarily by male critics with no particular allegiances to Love made disparaging the contents of the album a less compelling measure by which to fuel her growing mob of detractors. Because it was not acceptable to call the album a failure, rumors began to circulate that it was a forgery.

Word spread quickly from rock scene whispers and embryonic online forums that it was Kurt who had written the bulk of the album, despite the sworn and repeated word of those who witnessed the album's entire development and creation. Producer Paul Kolderie was present for the recording of *Live Through This* and noted, "He [Kurt] was very interested in what was going on, but I could tell that he wasn't behaving as someone would behave if he had created it himself, or if he knew the songs."[3] Numerous accounts affirm essentially the same story: Kurt seemed impressed by but unfamiliar with the songs. It also notably doesn't really sound like anything Kurt had written before. But this fact is attributed to Kurt's otherworldly genius and versatility—rather than Courtney's.

Courtney broke her silence over the issue in 1998, telling the *Observer*, "I mean for fuck's sake, his skills were much better than mine at the time—the songs would have been much better."[4] Her claim was entirely uncontroversial: It was taken for granted that Courtney was the lesser talent in the duo. But in revisiting Hole's work outside the immediate context of Kurt's death, critics have emerged to suggest a truth that might have been unseemly to print before this decade. "*Live Through This* is, in a lot of ways, a melodically sharper and more inviting album than anything Nirvana or Pearl Jam or Soundgarden were doing at the time," writes Tom Breihan on *StereoGum* in 2014.[5] Alex Galbraith writes on UPROXX in 2015 about how listening to Nirvana through the lens of "the Cult of Nirvana" obscures a very important point: A lot of their songs were self-pitying gibberish. "Hole had their fair share of angsty songs, but they always used that angst to shine a light outward. Both Love and Cobain wrote songs about intensely personal situations, but only the former couched her complaints in universal language," Galbraith writes.[6] But the large-scale public investment in despising Courtney would not let itself be devastated by the fact that she was talented. The audacity to be more brilliant than a fallen hero required punishment, so punish her they did. Courtney was the one who sang "I love him so much it just turns to hate," but those words could just as easily have been the motto of the hate mob that came for Courtney Love.

In the wild west of the early Internet, conspiracy theorists made the case for Courtney orchestrating Kurt's murder with often melodramatically named websites like "Justice for Kurt." Some still exist today on Tripod and Geocities mirror platforms. America Online had to delete a Hole forum on its platform in part due to a death threat sent to Courtney in 1995—a relative rarity at that time. And then there's the case of Tom Grant, the private investigator hired by Courtney to seek out information on Kurt's whereabouts when he would disappear amid the decline of their marriage. Grant turned against Courtney in the wake of Kurt's death after learning of evidence that he saw as indicative of a murder plot.

More than twenty years later, the struggle by some fans to get closer to Kurt via violence toward his family continued as recently as 2015. Frances Bean Cobain, who reported that a stalker had stayed in her home for three days while she was on vacation, said, "This person's twisted explanation was that he was meant to be with me because my father's soul had entered my body."[7] Though such unhinged behavior is rare, there are plenty of fans who have deified Kurt to the point of reducing his child to a sacred relic. And while Courtney still makes headlines on a semiregular basis, her daughter, Frances, has become the more sought-after spectacle of the Cobain tragedy.

Frances often appears gracious and accommodating during media appearances, in sharp contrast to her frequently evasive late father and notoriously combative mother. But you often have to look hard for Frances in every story in which she appears because writers still tend to veil her in the features of her father. And while she shares physical similarities with both of her striking parents, the public still insists on casting her as Kurt's beautiful shadow—ghoulishly demanding that she be like her father who died instead of the woman who insisted on living.

I tried to accept Courtney as the girl with the most cake for years, silently complicit in narratives that dismiss female rage as symptomatic of a juvenile character rather than the logical response to a hostile world. She was simply on a little rampage when she offered too many sexually explicit details about another rock star she had fucked. She didn't *mean* to be such an embarrassment or such a bitch all the time. But my own transformation from girl child to woman, and the attendant punishments from the world, saw my view of Courtney shift. I surmised that these were not the missteps of immaturity but the intentional humiliation of her detractors in a brilliant performance of ignorance that disguised her true malevolence. It is in these moments that I see Courtney's vicious bile as a rational reaction to the public's attempts to keep her on trial in perpetuity. Now when I conjure the outsized specter of Courtney as a venomous witch, I see the woman I aspire to be rather than the clumsy girl I have so often been.

I do not know if I was naturally inclined to trip over myself or if I was rendered this way. There was being labeled a tease by my sixth-grade teacher for holding hands with a boy whose grades weren't as good as mine. Or the time I was called a condescending cunt by a male friend because I told his drunk friend, in no uncertain terms, that he was out of line for saying he would love to hear the sound of his dick breaking my hymen. Or when at twenty-three I felt my own twisted sense of *gratitude* that the investment banker who raped me had abated when I pleaded that he not penetrate me anally. Or when my first sugar daddy held my head on his cock, not releasing it until he had fully ejaculated in my mouth and felt me swallow.

When I worked as a stripper, I regularly heard fantasies from male clients about running away with me, but these were really just stories about these men abandoning the women and children who relied on them. There might still be countless avatars of me being held hostage in the minds of men who would make me complicit in their callousness. For all the years that these vulgar haunts have lingered, so, too, has Courtney's mordant interrogation: "Was she asking for it? / Was she asking nice? / Yeah, she was asking for it / Did she ask you twice?" It goes to a low volume sometimes, but it is never turned all the way off.

Like Courtney, I have also had the personal misfortune of falling in love with a mild-mannered man whose massive love for me still paled in comparison to his love of heroin. He was two weeks out of rehab when I met him, and he was gentle and handsome, and while we were together I lived in constant fear that I would find him dead one day. Even now, after living for years without him, I wonder sometimes if he will die too young. He had an extended relapse in our years together, and I spent the season trying to conjure a heartbeat from the shadow he had become.

I have learned that I crave the myth of a formidable woman rather than a little girl rotting from the inside out, and the witchcraft at play on *Live Through This* is but one example of how Courtney always had a stronger taste for blood than for cake. The guiding image for this revision is Courtney devouring Kurt's heart. Courtney told *Vanity Fair* in 1995 that she had taken not just hair from Kurt's head, as was documented in *People* the year prior, but pubic hair as well. " 'I *wanted* his heart," she says. "I wanted his heart to put an oak in it."[8] She claimed that this is a Saxon tradition, but experts in medieval Saxon magic and folklore with whom I spoke had never heard of this ritual, though occult historians were quick to tell me that there are spells aplenty involving the extraction of a person's heart to access their power. The image of the wicked queen in *Snow White* demanding the beautiful child's heart delivered to her in a box comes to mind (Courtney was fittingly cast as this witch in a childhood production of the play). Mad with jealousy and rage that Snow White has survived in the wilderness, the queen transforms into a witch and hunts her down. Unfortunately, we are never clued in to how the queen was made wicked or if she was born that way. But a document trail through Courtney's past makes it possible to indulge in the wild speculation that the curses she breathed into the world were a long time coming.

In a 1998 biography of Courtney, Poppy Z. Brite describes how Courtney was called "Pee Girl" by her peers because she was notoriously unclean.[9] This was due to hygiene negligence in the commune where she lived. Her mother, Linda Carroll, told *Vanity Fair* that Courtney seemed to always be in physical pain, reacting to human touch with genuine suffering. Carroll also told *Vanity Fair* that Courtney had frequent nightmares and drew pictures of wounded figures while her peers scratched away at butterflies.[10] Courtney told *Spin* in 1995, "I forever looked like I was seven. And then I got ugly; I was ugly until I was 25. But back then, I was usually one of the most attractive people in the room, except in an unusual way. Still, I knew what I had, and I worked the fuck out of it. And so when it was gone I really missed it."[11] A sensitive, beautiful child suddenly cursed with ugliness and tortured by ghastly dreams is an origin story that lends credence to both black magic practice and perhaps an equally unforgivable crime: mortal ascent to power through female cunning.

The vanishing of Courtney's beauty was among the least of her worries in a childhood characterized by frenzy and motion. "It was autumn in San Francisco, the season of the witch, 1964" is how the legend begins in Brite's biography. Her father, Hank, was already ambivalent about his pregnant wife, Linda, who "nurtured her fetus in a heady broth of fear and sugar" as she was drawn to sweets but increasingly repulsed by her own reflection. The prenatal potion in which Courtney was forged was the first of many odd pairings in her early life: a cripplingly attached mother who was hopelessly inept at child care, and a mostly negligent father who gathered his attention together for Courtney just long enough to dose her with LSD at the age of four, a claim that her father denies. After her parents' divorce, she was shuffled around the globe, her life spent with a network of friends and relatives and punctuated by time in boarding schools and in the juvenile justice system. Brite's biography features detailed reports from the institutions where she stayed. Her disruptive anger and penchant for obscenity make frequent appearances, but the most consistent remarks are about Courtney's exceptional intelligence and her chillingly brilliant imagination. "Courtney dreamed about keeping tiny people in jars and starving them, about starting a farm for women where she would beat them and make them beautiful" is among the more colorful descriptions from Courtney's otherworldly mind.[12]

The 1980s were Courtney's stumbling apprenticeship through social climbing that prepared her for the more ambitious scaling she would perform in her wicked prime during the '90s. "Kurt Cobain and Courtney Love first locked eyes on each other at eleven in the evening on Friday, January 12, 1990, and within 30 seconds they were tussling on the floor" is how Charles R. Cross introduces their courtship in *Heavier Than Heaven: A Biography of Kurt Cobain*.[13] Both have infamous eyes: Courtney's were described in *Spin* in 1994 as "perpetually startled blue eyes capable of great ferocity," while the "cornflower blue" of Kurt's eyes is well-documented.[14] Michael Stipe recalled during Nirvana's Rock and Roll Hall of Fame induction, "The first time I looked into his eyes I just went, 'I get it. He is all that. He is a very special person.' "[15] This fact did not go unnoticed by Courtney. "He was super cute but he carried himself like someone who didn't know it. That was part of the charm," Courtney would later recall in the documentary *Kurt Cobain: Montage of Heck*.[16]

A fan who attended a 1992 show at Australian National University told music critic Anwen Crawford about seeing Courtney on the side of the stage. "I couldn't take my eyes off her, because she was transfixed on him. It was such a romantic, fucked up, rock 'n' roll thing."[17] "By far the most frequently mentioned physical distinction of the witch was the possession of unusual eyes or an uncanny gaze," Professor Owen Davies writes in *Witchcraft, Magic and Culture, 1736–1951*.[18] Operative witchcraft manuals frequently refer to witches training to fix their gazes on objects or persons in order to manipulate or control them. What if Courtney was not projecting a signal of infatuation with Kurt but siphoning his psychic energy, his genius, *his very will to live* with her gaze?

Like a bird accidentally crushed in the hands of a child, it is tempting to blame their unraveling on intemperate love rather than actual malice. Details of their courtship read like those of precocious goth teenagers: He gave her a heart-shaped box full of dolls that looked like dead children; they exchanged love letters characterized by mutual devotion that would read as saccharine if you cut out all the allusions to death. In *Montage of Heck*, there is a sequence showing the two clearly strung out, playing with children's toys in their filthy apartment and exchanging loving non sequiturs. "Why do you think that everyone thinks that you're the good one and I'm the bad one," Courtney wonders aloud. "Because I know how to use my illusion," Kurt replies, a clever play on *Use Your Illusion*, the album title of Kurt's chosen nemesis, Guns N' Roses front man Axl Rose. He says this with clarity, but it is ultimately without meaning. It is a turn of phrase that seems like it was pulled from some more ancient, prescient literary source but is every bit a piece of 1990s hollowness imbued with more profundity than it holds.

Later in the film, Kurt appears wearing what looks like some combination of a prom dress and a communion dress, a black rectangle taped over his lip slightly longer than a Hitler mustache. As Courtney reads an angry letter written to *Sassy* magazine by an irate reader calling herself "Stacy, the Kurt Slave," Kurt moves his mouth to keep rhythm with Courtney's reading, miming the outrage of the reader and gleefully submitting to being a literal puppet for Courtney. The performance is meant as a mockery of Stacy, who is incensed that the magazine printed a feature about both of them rather than just about Kurt, but the humiliation is entirely Kurt's here. The gag is at once mean-spirited toward the teen girl at which it is directed and humiliating to Kurt himself as he performs it.

Kurt's behavior during their relationship is a study in surrendering control of one's identity. Concert footage in *Montage of Heck* shows Kurt standing onstage in front of thousands and lamenting that Courtney thinks people hate her. He then commands them to shout, "Courtney, we love you." The crowd obeys him without hesitation, submitting to the disgrace of professing love for a woman they believed to be destroying him. Kurt writes in a note to Courtney, "Fuck of all fucks, let me live forever with you." He not only exalts her, he seeks permission to take his own breath. "I love you more than my mother. I would abort Christ for you. I'll make myself miserable to make you happy," he writes in another letter. But mere submission to her brutality would not do; Courtney required his commitment to an all-out war on God. And he certainly made good on the promise.

After Kurt overdosed in Rome in early March 1994, Kurt and Courtney returned to Seattle, where they had a series of fights that were occasionally punctuated by urgent calls to their lawyers. Kurt wanted a divorce and to write Courtney out of his will. Courtney responded (and I'm ad-libbing here), "The fuck you are." Kurt was apparently preoccupied with the circumstances of the overdose, and Courtney staged an intervention—that peculiarly empathetic yet humiliating ritual extended to addicts believed to be at or nearing rock bottom. It is a cleansing surrender for those who truly are and a brutal mind game to those who are not. In either case, Kurt was disempowered. And he wasn't an especially powerful boy to begin with.

Courtney retreated to the Peninsula Hotel in Beverly Hills the next day to promote her forthcoming album. It was a cold move certainly, though more negligent than cruel. Kurt and his best friend, Dylan Carlson, went to buy a shotgun, for self-defense according to Carlson. People do not, of course, necessarily announce their trigger-sad intentions when they buy their suicide weapons, so who is to say, really? And though there is a case to be made for his fear being of Courtney's hired goons, it is worth noting that he had the kind of fans who later believed he had transubstantiated into his infant daughter and was awaiting their companionship upon her reaching adulthood. That he didn't have a shotgun earlier is among the bigger shocks of the story, really.

It is here in the early spring, on the eve of a masterpiece being unleashed on the world, that Courtney, the previously merely greedy bitch, is most gloriously reimagined into an otherworldly instrument of madness and death. Kurt checked into the Exodus Recovery Center in Los Angeles on March 30. He stayed only two days before dramatically scaling the six-foot walls of the center despite being free to walk out the front gate. Why did he choose a method of escape when he could simply exit? Why did he return to Seattle and believe for a moment that he could go undetected under baggy jackets and large sunglasses? When Kurt left the center, Courtney sent a private investigator to Seattle to find him. One cannot help but think of Snow White believing she had avoided death when the huntsman took pity on her, only to find that she was still being doggedly pursued by a far greater evil. And just as Snow White bites into the apple of her own volition, Kurt likely pulled the trigger himself. "Some day you will ache like I ache" was a promise Courtney made good on.

Though I heard the murder rumors with everyone else in the first few years after Kurt's death, Nick Broomfield's 1998 documentary, *Kurt and Courtney*, was my first deep dive into any serious meditation on the possibility of foul play. An especially memorable scene involves a wild-eyed musician nicknamed "El Duce" claiming Courtney asked him to "whack" Kurt for $50,000 but that his friend did it instead. Despite his violent claims, the Duce's bald head and doughy features come together to make him look like an overgrown but decidedly ugly baby, and he was killed by a train three days after he made his on-camera claims that Courtney wanted him to serve as her personal assassin.

In conjuring various iterations of Courtney the witch, I return often to her doll-infested homes and lyrics. The tradition of the voodoo doll and a number of other magical practices claim a person can summon death to a human target via a toy likeness and a sufficiently robust will to power. The magic books I consulted all warn that most death spells fail because of insufficient power by the casting witch or magician. But surely if the spirits would obey any kind of person, the demonic heiress to a rock legend drenched in blood would be it.

I realize, of course, that the cruel and supernatural Courtney Love I have fashioned in my mind is a fiction. She was born in the vulgar imaginations of those who felt they were more entitled to Kurt Cobain's beating heart than the woman whose body bore his only child. I also realize that the image of Courtney on trial is easy to imbue with meaning given knowledge of the events that would occur after the recording of *Live Through This*. But I am hardly the first person to retroactively assign symbols to events in the Pacific Northwest in the early 1990s because I had a point to make. When discussing Kurt and Courtney with my best friend Phoebe, she summed up my feelings perfectly when she said, "Look, I don't think Courtney killed Kurt," then she paused a moment to grin and continued, "But I think it would be pretty fucking cool if she did." And because Courtney herself has made no secret of her desire to attain the status of a legend, I entertain these absurd possibilities as a celebration of female brutality rather than the typical condemnation of it.

When given a choice between the girl with the most cake and the liar at the witch trial, I choose the witch every time. I prefer Courtney as the ancient sorceress convincing the public of her innocence. The disguise of the lost little girl who sabotages her own attempts to gain approval by dissolving into tantrums is a sufficiently degenerate cover for something truly sinister. I like Courtney the succubus, Courtney the bitch. I revel in the idea of Courtney as the thief of men's genius and as the employer of assassins.

When evil is done to a person, it gets under their skin. If there is enough of it, it'll sink down through the flesh and into the bones, becoming part of its target. For most of us, the pain is absorbed as poison rather than power. We see a world awash in women's blood and tears. We endure claims that the most profound kinds of pain are the exclusive possessions of men, that they are best equipped to make art from this suffering. Instead of bearing witness to it, we are asked to be killed by it, quietly if possible. But Courtney did nothing quietly. She said in 1995, "The American public really does have a death wish for me. They want me to die. I'm not going to die."[19] And she has made good on that promise. The word "survivor" comes up often in sympathetic profiles of her. But "survivor" has connotations of thriving, of some conquering of life's wreckage rather than a dwelling in it. Witches do not survive; they simply refuse to die.

In the witch trials of seventeenth-century New England, authorities would put the accused in water and use her flotation as evidence of rejecting baptism—and she would submerge just enough to get them to pull her back to shore. They would strip her naked in search of demonic markings, only to find flawless flesh where a pox had been rumored. They would throw her into a rushing river and she would fucking swim. And perhaps most fittingly, cakes were baked from the rye meal, the ashes, and the urine or blood of victims and fed to a dog. If the dog exhibited signs of bewitchment, it was considered evidence that witchcraft was at play. But unlike the unwitting dogs of this coarse ritual, the human public actively consumed the blood and detritus of Kurt and fell willingly enchanted. We are never sated in our appetite for that which would destroy itself. It is we who are offered a taste and beg for more.

The rituals by which we humiliate women have migrated from folklore-inspired trials of the body to more sterile but no less degrading assassinations of character. Courtney foretold their brutality before enduring it herself. I have lived in this world that she warned us girls about. I have loved the kind of man who loved only certain things because he loved to see them break, to borrow a phrase. I have not seen a fraction of the cruelty that the world is capable of, but I have trembled often enough in the aftershocks of my own resistance to a world built to break me to know that female brutality is not just an acceptable response, it is the most sensible one, too. But my heart is home to docile rage because I am afraid: afraid I don't know how to wield my own viciousness with any expertise and afraid that once I do know how, I won't stop until the fire I set can be seen from space. This is why in my personal mythology of Courtney, she has mastered not only the art of the supernatural foul play necessary to wreak havoc on the world, but the practical skills of restraint and deception that elevate such magic. The end result is a world begging for the mercy of a deathless woman, and her grinning reply that they were asking for it.

Our Sisters Shall
Inherit the Sky

On the Lisbon Sisters and the
Misnomer of *The Virgin Suicides*

B EFORE I READ *THE VIRGIN SUICIDES*, I read about how
Josh Hartnett asked Kirsten Dunst to her prom—at the
bidding of Sofia Coppola, who was directing them both in the
film adaptation of the book. I came across the story flipping
through back issues of *Seventeen* magazine while I was taking
PE as a summer school course. I was at once resentful and
enamored. It was a Hollywood anecdote sticky with charm,
from the fact that teen actress Dunst had a confidante in the
young director Coppola, to Hartnett the heartthrob with
a heart of gold being a good sport and asking his younger
costar to the dance.

Dunst ultimately chose to skip the prom entirely, baffling
and devastating my fifteen-year-old self. I could not get a

date of any kind, much less one with a highly desirable movie star four years my senior. I saw myself as the inheritor of bad genes that rendered me thicker than my peers and destined for a cruelly obscure suburban existence. And this feeling only sank deeper when faced with Dunst's decision to opt out of a coveted role in the important social ritual of prom. I blamed what I decided was her effortless thinness and only mildly deserved fame. I silently hurled unfair and inaccurate assumptions at her charmed life, foisting my inadequacy at her in accusations she would never hear.

At the end of the summer, my sister Nova and I went to see *The Virgin Suicides* in a small movie theater in downtown San Diego when it finally found its way into cities beyond New York and Los Angeles. It was still a gamble on Nova's part to take me to an R-rated movie because she had to buy my ticket and then hope against hope that I would not be asked for an ID at the ticket counter. But Nova was inclined then and is inclined even now to believe in the magical properties of sisterhood, that there was something about blood and secrets and being girls that elevated us. My sister and I were born on the same date three years apart under the sign of Gemini, the twins. Our shared birthday and the particular star sign have given a cosmic edge to our sisterhood that I am sure all sisters share, but I have the benefit of real mythology to back it up.

Greek mythology is scattered with clusters of sisters who offer moral instruction, and I have infused our own origin story with similar cosmic heft for my entire life. My sister, too, was preoccupied with the stars; one year she cut out a gold foil star and glued it to a blue cardboard block the size of a playing card and wrote a message on the back of it, dedicating a star to me. And so it was no surprise that Nova, whose name means "star," took in the melancholy '99 tribute to teenage tedium alongside me, whose name means "child," with above-average levels of youthful despair and recognition. Though Josh Hartnett was the designated dreamboat of the film as Trip Fontaine, it was the five girls playing the Lisbon sisters with whom I was distraught to part ways when the credits rolled.

Hanna R. Hall appears on-screen as the living Cecilia only for a few minutes, but she makes an enchanting specter in appearances later on. Of all the Lisbon sisters, she had the most courage in her conviction that death was the appropriate response to life as it had been handed to her. Hall had played the child version of Jenny in *Forrest Gump* five years earlier, so when she jumped to her death in *The Virgin Suicides*, I could not help but recall the failure of her prayer from the earlier film, "Dear God, make me a bird so I can fly far, far, far away." It failed this time, too.

My anger at Dunst for turning down Hartnett melted as she retreated into the character of Lux, the fourteen-year-old Lisbon sister whose disaffectedness seems to spread the suicide contagion most aggressively in the household. Chelse Swain plays Bonnie, the sister I later learned was characterized by a sharp nose, a long neck, and substantial height in Jeffrey Eugenides's book. Swain possessed none of these markers, but she was the lesser-known sister of Dominique Swain, an actress made famous briefly in the late 1990s and early 2000s, and so it seemed especially fitting that she was the lost middle sister. A. J. Cook plays Mary, who was the most vain of the Lisbon sisters, and when animated by Cook's lovely smile and gentle features, it is easy to see why. Therese, the most awkward and intellectual sister, is played by Leslie Hayman, who never appeared in another film but who looked like a popular girl from my high school and so will always be famous to me. I bought the novel the following day and envisioned the Lisbon sisters as the girls who brought them to life on-screen, and I have never been able to separate the two.

I devoured the sedulously constructed dreamscape of Eugenides's debut novel as only a fantasizing teenager would. That I could be so easily convinced of the sex appeal of suburban Detroit in 1974 is both a credit to the book's artful prose and an indicator of how green I thought grass was on the other side of wherever I stood. The story is narrated by a group of grown men who as boys were infatuated with the five Lisbon sisters, a brood of peculiar blond teen girls, and who, from the boys' perspective, were composed almost entirely of feminine mysteries and reedy limbs. Following the suicide of the youngest sister, Cecilia, the girls begin a retreat from the world that eventually culminates in all four of the remaining sisters killing themselves. There are plenty of events in between these deaths: a homecoming dance, lots of sex on the Lisbon household roof, a protest against an ongoing municipal tree removal project, and several phone calls consisting entirely of records playing rather than people speaking. But at its core, the story is fan fiction about girls the boys could never really hope to know.

The Virgin Suicides is also a lie, starting with the title and running through to the very last words. Of the five Lisbon sisters who die by their own hands, there is at least one confirmed loss of virginity and plenty of subsequent sex. The speculative fiction begins soon after in the retelling of Cecilia's first suicide attempt, but grows more glaring in the lead-up to a party that the Lisbons throw in order to cheer up Cecilia, the reluctant survivor of her own slashed wrists. The men narrating the story are positively horny at the memory of receiving handmade construction-paper invitations to the party. "It was thrilling to know that the Lisbon girls knew our names, that their delicate vocal cords had pronounced their syllables, and that they meant something in their lives. They had had to labor over proper spellings and to check our addresses in the phone book or by the metal numbers nailed to the trees." The boys are invited to a party that is designed to save a thirteen-year-old girl's life, and they deduce that it was their names and addresses the sisters labored over most meticulously in their planning. If the sisters believe that drowning out the call of oblivion that beckons their baby sister toward death with party music is at least a close second, they do not say as much. Cecilia kills herself in the middle of the party, which one might think would render the boys gentler with the objects of their affection. One might think.

Instead, they write of a more urgent obsession: "In the first few days after the funeral, our interest in the Lisbon girls only increased. Added to their loveliness was a new mysterious suffering, perfectly silent, visible in the blue puffiness beneath their eyes or the way they would sometimes stop in mid stride, look down, and shake their heads as though disagreeing with life. Grief made them wander." As the Lisbon girls develop ever-stranger wanderings of mind and body, the boys obsess more actively about their interior lives and speculate accordingly.

I recall a craving to be precisely this kind of object of infatuation when I was a teenager reading the book. I wanted a boy to look at me and see the mystery of my suffering and, instead of being repulsed by my emotions, to want to draw closer, to know more. But what the boys call observation feels much more like surveillance when rereading the text. My teen misery was mostly of my own making, a nagging sense of being incomplete but without any tangible loss to justify such feelings. The boys' preoccupation is with the very private grief of losing one of your own. I know that as an adult woman, I should forgive the indelicate ways teen boys treat teen girls, even in their own speculations. I know, too, that they are fictions dissecting fictions. And yet I cannot stop myself from becoming fifteen again, staring down the prospect of a whole lifetime ahead of me without my sister and not screaming at the crude and incompetent analysis that would understate the loss of my sister, the girl whom even my infant self wanted to emulate so badly that I snatched her birthday. She is no less a part of me than my own beating heart. As an adult woman, I am eager to protect young girls from these crude and incompetent analyses, even if they are fictions dissecting fictions.

Though the boys never admit as much, it is crucial that the Lisbon sisters are all thin and beautiful within reason. There are a handful of imperfect features among them but nothing that would make the sum of each one's parts less than desirable. In the safety of being attractive, their eccentricities are as precious as their bodies. Their bodies protect all eccentricity from becoming "strange" or "gross" in the way similar predilections are characterized when possessed by heavier or uglier girls. From the distance at which the boys spy on them, everything about the girls is a source of fascination. They are blank canvases onto which they can project their own stories of perfect love and trust and see it reflected back at them.

These half-formed ideations are flawless because they are incomplete, perfect only because they are so ill-conceived. The girls are mysterious but long to be known. They are (mostly) chaste, but they also crave. And above all, they are dead. And dead girls don't write stories. The last year of the Lisbon sisters' lives is instead governed on paper by the wandering imaginations of boys at their periphery—or, rather, the men the boys become. They narrate the story of the girls as a group of adults loving what they couldn't have, seeing the sisters only from the distances between suburban windows and adjacent lockers. The men who narrate are softened by their surrender to age and hardened to the women they married for having aged into the fullness of living real human lives. They resent these women for forcing them to reckon with the full humanity of women in a way that the dreamy Lisbon sisters never forced them to. The Lisbon sisters died before they ever came close enough to reveal their second and third dimensions. Boys often have permission to become men without the forfeiture of their desirability. And so these men write stories that grasp at girls who are phantoms twice over: first by being dead and second by being shallow shadows of actual girls, the assorted fragments of men's aging imaginations rather than the deep and dimensioned creatures that real girls are.

The turning point in the novel is when Lux has sex with Trip Fontaine after homecoming, prompting her mother to withdraw the girls from all interaction outside the house that will become their catacomb. Lux begins taking lovers on the roof of the Lisbon house under cover of night while her beleaguered but loyal sisters keep watch. The boys take this as an opportunity for off-label sex education. "For our own part, we learned a great deal about the techniques of love, and because we didn't know the words to denote what we saw, we had to make up our own. That was why we spoke of 'yodeling in the canyon' and 'tying the tube,' of 'groaning in the pit,' 'slipping the turtle's head,' and 'chewing the stinkweed,'" they explain. This is perhaps meant to demonstrate their juvenility but inadvertently betrays the extent of their surveillance. That is a lot of sex acts to have witnessed.

The boys' voyeuristic impulses leave not so much an impression as a wound. "Years later, when we lost our own virginities, we resorted in our panic to pantomiming Lux's gyrations on the roof so long ago; and even now, if we were to be honest with ourselves, we would have to admit that it is always that pale wraith we make love to," they write, apparently unashamed that they fantasize about fucking a fourteen-year-old on the brink of death. They do not see Lux's sex rampage as an act of desperation, the frantic search by a young person to find her own pulse. Or so I can hope. The alternative is that they see the desperation of a broken child with perfect clarity and still find it arousing.

More dreadful still is the fact that the boys track down the men with whom Lux had her starlit dalliances, and they are all inexplicably ready to chat about fucking a fourteen-year-old and revel in the memories of her figure, diminished at this point by what sounds like anorexia. "All sixteen mentioned her jutting ribs, the insubstantiality of her thighs, and one, who went up to the roof with Lux during a warm winter rain, told us how the basins of her collarbones collected water," the narrators report. I read this and longed to physically disappear from the world so that I might psychically reappear in the male imagination as Lux did, her body defined by its absences rather than its substance. It is perfect because it is not much of anything at all. As someone with naturally deep wells on either side of my clavicle that have been made more hollow by disordered eating from time to time, I knew that ears obstruct rain from pooling there, and lying down would make the rain slide down and out. But it didn't make the idea of gathering the rain with my hunger any less appealing. I think back to the girl I was in high school, reading these passages and wanting so badly to be Lux Lisbon *specifically* that I could not see how much I was like her generally.

I did not consider the possibility that I was imprinting as a one-dimensional memory on the men in their mid-twenties who took me to parties where they'd fill me with drugs and alcohol and tell me how different I was from other girls my age. On midnight excursions I'd go on with such men to the beaches of the southernmost points of San Diego, we'd remark in drunken stupors on nonsensical things like how the lights from nearby Tijuana, Mexico, did not reflect the language barrier that our border did and proceed to kiss for hours under their illumination. And yet in the throes of these melancholy and impossibly young dalliances with men and mortality, I still saw my life as pedestrian and Lux's as so cerebral.

Drawing the boys into the rotting home that they will soon vacate in body bags is an even greater victory for the girls than the suicides themselves. The boys think they are invited to the Lisbon home the night of their planned suicides to help the girls run away with them. The girls reply that they would literally rather die by dying. The unlucky and beautiful Mary survives her attempt to gas herself in the oven and must endure a dreadful month of sleeping and six-times-daily showers before joining her sisters in suicide with a mouthful of sleeping pills. The town awaits her death with the self-interested disposition of vultures.

"In the end we had the pieces of the puzzle, but no matter how we put them together, gaps remained, oddly shaped emptinesses mapped by what surrounded them, like countries we couldn't name," the men declare, as they acknowledge their bafflement by the riddle of the Lisbon sisters when they take inventory of the evidence they gathered in the months and years that followed. "The girls took into their own hands decisions better left to God. They became too powerful to live among us, too self-concerned, too visionary, too blind," the men say, dwelling on what they felt they lost the night of June 15 when the remaining four sisters executed their grand self-executions.

But the Lisbon sisters knew exactly what happened when decisions were left to God. Their own mother's hypervigilance was born of godly instruction and culminated in the girls' residential incarceration; the physical decay of their home as its upkeep was neglected grew more unbearable than even death. And to speak of girls in these circumstances as "too powerful" and "too self-concerned" demonstrates the nearsightedness of these men's entitlement. It is when the men refer to "the outrageousness of a human being thinking only of herself" that it is most clear they had not learned a thing about their alluring neighbors in the intervening decades. In all that time, they never seemed to realize that the impenetrability of the Lisbon fortress was made possible by the bonds of sisterhood the boys could never hope to penetrate.

The phrase "Lisbon girls" appears in the book fifty-six times. Surprisingly, the phrase "Lisbon sisters" does not appear once. The boys did not seek out the points at which the sisters' lives intersected, those ties that felt like simple family structure at times and like the binding of the cosmos at others. Anyone with siblings knows that these strange and infuriating creatures with whom we share blood and shelter inform our interior lives more than anyone else, both during childhood and, for some of us, even once we have escaped it. To lose a sibling is to feel mortality closer at hand than in any other death. The suicides were not individual acts of selfishness but a collective act of grief. They grieved over the death of their youngest sister, Cecilia, but they also grieved for one another, seeing flickers of themselves reflected in each other's faces and recognizing the pain of inheriting an ungentle world that was second in its torment only to the pain of being cloistered away from it.

Siblings are the first people we love irrationally. Their faces and behaviors are like funhouse-mirror versions of our own, formed into different configurations of the same genetic material, but eerily similar to our own. It is similarity but not duplication that renders sisters capable of the envy and competition for which they are well-known. But sisters also share the strange fate of being carriers of their family's genes but often not of their family's name, particularly in a Catholic family in the 1970s Midwest. Together they inherit the tradition of womanhood that asks them to fold quietly into the family histories of men. They must surrender much of that which bound them to those they first loved so they can contribute to the immortality project of some other name. Their tenderness toward one another is a function of knowing their finitude as members of the unit into which they were born and inside which they first loved.

No sister in her right mind would willingly draw her sisters closer to the call of death alongside her. Sisters want each other to live. But the Lisbon sisters are not in their right minds. They are driven mad by the knowledge that they are being obsessed over by boys who cannot and should not know them because the boys have neither their interest nor their consent. They respond to this obsession and the self-aggrandizement that makes the boys think they can save the Lisbon sisters by luring them into the promise of exile but deliver only cold reminders of the body's borders at mortality. The boys are traumatized not by the deaths of the girls but by their own impotence. "It didn't matter in the end how old they had been, or that they were girls, but only that we had loved them, and that they hadn't heard us calling, still do not hear us, up here in the tree house, with our thinning hair and soft bellies, calling them out of those rooms where they went to be alone for all time, alone in suicide, which is deeper than death, and where we will never find the pieces to put them back together," they recall in the book's last lines. But the Lisbon sisters heard them loud and clear. They simply declined their offers.

Though Jeffrey Eugenides's second novel, *Middlesex*, makes rich use of Greek mythology, it is strangely absent from *The Virgin Suicides*, where I think it would find kindred spirits. The Pleiades are the seven daughters of Atlas and Pleione who have the misfortune of catching Orion's eye, leading him to fall in love with them and pursue them across the earth. The gods take pity on them and turn all seven first into doves and then into stars. The seven stars are situated in the sky next to Orion, forever fatigued by his pursuit. There are dozens of variations on this myth, but all center on a unit of girls too grief-stricken to carry on without a member of their family. Without a title like widow or orphan to name the grief of losing siblings, their corpses cascade onto each other in an unknowable and unnamed sorrow.

It is in the variations of these myths scattered around the world that it becomes clear the weight of the heavens was borne not by a man but by a group of young girls. Even as one myself, I invested so much anger in a girl whom I did not know but on whom I laid the weight of many of my own sorrows. I was baffled at the prospect of rejecting an opportunity to be seen because I did not yet know the curse of being seen without also being known. I think of the love of Trip Fontaine for Lux, which was described as "truer than all subsequent loves because it never had to survive." And then I think of my sister, whose love will survive whether I want it to or not. I think of the stars we were born under, the peculiar pain of inheriting and the particular joy of sharing it from time to time. And then I think of the foil star she gave me when we were girls. It is faded and worn thin now but bears celestial weight in its meaning: She believed I had a right to own a piece of the heavens alongside her. And though the boys look at the Lisbon artifacts like the oddly shaped emptiness of countries they cannot name, I look at the clearly defined shape of my artifact and know that sisters are not to be confined to the finitude of nations but freed to the eternity of the stars.

Broken-Bodied Girls

On the Horror of Little Girls Grown

WATCHING HORROR FILMS AS A child was primarily an exercise in witnessing the injured inflict more injuries. Freddy Krueger's body is a giant burn that doesn't heal. The only kindness ever extended by Jason Voorhees over the last three decades has been to cover his deformed head with a hockey mask. The eerily symmetrical torture inflicted on Pinhead's skull on display in *Hellraiser* was less merciful. But while these ghoulish men frightened me out of more nights of rest than my mother can likely count, they never inspired the same inconsolable terror that would reverberate in me after encountering the disfigured young girls of the genre— notably, Regan from *The Exorcist* and the lesser-known but far more gruesome Zelda from *Pet Sematary*.

Most men in horror movies show no evidence of having ever been children. While a perfunctory nod is given to

Jason as a child victim in the first *Friday the 13th* film, the bloodthirsty adult is too unsympathetic to render his backstory much more than an afterthought. But we meet Regan as a bright-eyed adolescent whose innocent tinkering with a Ouija board was hardly sufficient vice to invite the brutal possession that followed. In *Pet Sematary*, Zelda is introduced in her sister Rachel's painful memory of being left by their parents to care for her in the excruciating stages of advanced spinal meningitis. Unlike their adult male counterparts, a major focal point of their respective stories was the girls as victims before they were villains. Growing up, I was afraid of running into Freddy or Jason in a dark alley or a nightmare, but I was more afraid of *becoming* Regan or Zelda.

I watched each of these movies at least a dozen times and so find it difficult to pinpoint my inaugural viewings. The sleepovers and all-nighters I pulled with my older sister bleed into one another and blur what might have indeed been revelatory moments. But my horror-bingeing definitely hit its peak (or its rock bottom, depending on your chosen addiction model) in the sixth grade, that especially cruel point in youth at which half the girls have crossed over into puberty while the other half have remained behind. Both groups are humiliated by belonging to their respective camp, indulging in misguided fantasies that the grass might be green anywhere on the landscape of early adolescence.

Even at age eleven, I knew *The Exorcist* was more than a chronicle of the terrible things that happen when you dabble in games of the occult. It was about sacrifice and faith, innocence lost, and the human body as the battleground for good and evil. Regan's possession demonstrated the latter in a series of progressively more ruinous and humiliating bodily changes. Her voice grows unrecognizable. Her body is subjected to violent and uncontrollable flailing. Her head memorably twists fully around, defying the generally rigid laws of the spinal cord. In the twenty-fifth-anniversary rerelease, a previously cut scene of Regan's body contorted into an insect-like pose and scampering down a flight of stairs found its way into new nightmares. These physical disfigurements are mirrored by her descent into moral disfigurement, punctuated by memorably profane proclamations like "Your mother sucks cock in hell!"

Though *Pet Sematary* mercifully spares its audience from a lot of screen time with Zelda, the particular horror of her disease leaves an indelible mark. "She started to look like this monster," her sister Rachel recalls through tears; Zelda's entire spine and rib cage are revealed through withering skin as she lurches toward her frightened sister. She is at once pitiful and terrifying, her expression pained as her head turns 360 degrees and she gurgles a cry for her sister's help. Zelda chokes to death in this scene and returns only as a gruesome and vengeful specter that warns, "I'm coming for you, Rachel, and this time, I'll get you." Her spinal disfigurement is healed in death, but the harshness of her prominent bones remains as she screeches, "I'm going to twist your back like mine so you'll never get out of bed again! Never get out of bed again! Never get out of bed again!" She lets out a sinister cackle at the amusing prospect of such torture being inflicted on a loved one.

The Scary Little Girl is at this point a tired horror cliché thrown haphazardly into films to draw foreshadowing pictures with crayons and allude to voices that adults cannot hear. But Regan and Zelda were frightening not because of eerie childlike qualities but because of monstrous adult ones. Their disfiguring physical transformations saw these once-innocent girls become sexual and ruthless in Regan's case and pitiless and manipulative in Zelda's. They were the victims of possession and disease that first incapacitated their bodies and then deformed their innocence, polluting childhood values with outsized variations on adult ones.

There is a third girl who haunts me, too, but not because of any physical scars making me cringe at the prospect of the pain at their origin points. It is instead the speed at which her body transforms both literally and figuratively from an emblem of innocence into a vessel of unadulterated evil. That girl is the title character in *Carrie*, an ostracized, harmless teen whose traumatic first menstrual period occurs in the film's memorable opening scene, a harbinger of the outpouring of blood that will soon be unleashed on her the night of the prom. "They're all gonna laugh at you," her mother warned, predicting that Carrie would endure that universal adolescent nightmare that is far worse than being drenched in pig's blood. When they do laugh at her, her heretofore unfocused telekinetic power has a purpose: to slaughter everyone in sight, laughing or not. Though Carrie's mother is remembered as a religious psychotic, her belief that it was nothing short of satanic influence that gave Carrie the powers is not so far from our culture's approach to the process of girls growing out of childhood. Little girls are good until they touch sin, at which point they grow ravenous for the stuff.

The great solace of the sleepover was the opportunity for a welcome retreat from negotiating my value in the presence of newly established bodily assets like breasts and new bends in my profile where there had once been straight lines. But the films we watched at them were stark reminders of the impending threat of adolescent change that would render our bodies unrecognizable, despite our protests, and in turn, transform our moral understanding of the world. It is easy to reject spiteful thoughts in a social environment not set about with the romance and ambition that plague the teen years. It is easy to reject the unseemliness of sex when you don't live in a body that is physically prepared to engage in it. But once the body is prepared to gestate new life, the genre told me, the body is also ready to bring destruction and even death. When a girl's body retreats so that a woman's can take its place, it is ready to betray the innocent mind still inside it as it grows more amenable to the latent evil that was waiting to be unlocked the entire time.

The horror genre is awash in male villains whose primarily facial disfigurements are thinly veiled metaphors for the moral disfigurements that prompt them to violently terrorize their victims. But it was these broken-bodied girls who haunted me well into adulthood as fracture points between the innocence of youth and the moral decay of adulthood. The border ran in a jagged, bloody line across the screen as we watched in transfixed terror in the darkened living rooms and basement rec rooms of our youth, the screen cruelly offering light but no salvation.

Charlotte in Exile

A Case for the Liberation of Scarlett Johansson from *Lost in Translation*

THE OFFICIAL WEBSITE FOR THE 2003 film *Lost in Translation* remained live and intact at the beginning of 2016, well over a decade after the film was released.[1] The central image is a still photo of a disheveled Bill Murray, sitting on a hotel room bed, looking into the camera. He is schlumpy and morose in a bathrobe and slippers, his hairline deeply receded. A much smaller still image of Scarlett Johansson standing outside in the Tokyo rain is offset to his left with her gazing in the direction of Murray. The alignment is such that if you follow her path of vision, it is actually at his shoulder, but the creative intention is clear. Below her image is the film's tagline, "Everyone wants to be found," in an uninspired font. At the bottom of the page is the claim, "Over 245 Critics Nationwide Rave 'ONE OF THE BEST

PICTURES OF THE YEAR!' more than any other movie of 2003" next to an appeal to buy the sound track on CD.

It is in some ways a charming artifact of a time in the early millennium before user experience was meticulously accounted for and when movie trailers took longer than milliseconds to upload, offering a sense of reward when they finally rolled. In other ways, it feels prescient for how people would come to understand the film years after its filters and afterglows had worn off. Though I'm sure it was not intended, it captured in amber what the film was about at its core. *Everyone wants to be found.* It is a true and incomplete thought. People want to be found, yes. Most of us long to be discovered, seen, and known by another. Despite those 245 critics gushing over the film as a simple but poignant portrayal of isolation giving way to friendship, I cannot help but see the asymmetry of that discovery. To me, the site reads the same way the film does: There is a peripheral woman who finds an important man. She looks at him longingly despite any apparent thing about him to long for. When I watched the film at the age of eighteen, I felt cheated that this was the sort of man I was supposed to be satisfied, even excited, was coming to find me.

That first viewing of *Lost in Translation* was characterized by boredom and bewilderment. Though I was not yet radicalized into wild hopes for a world of gender equity and I still harbored fantasies of saving undeserving men from themselves, I still felt as if something was amiss. My male peers ogled Johansson in the role of Charlotte, her first shot on-screen famously being a close-up of her ass. To lust after her was indeed their right, even their obligation. Charlotte's loveliness and soft-spoken wit are in sharp contrast to her absentee traveling companion, a vapid celebrity photographer husband who is based loosely on Coppola's ex-husband, director Spike Jonze. Johansson was stunning in the film, and she remains so today. For those of us who came of age around the turn of the millennium, Johansson embodied ideals of beauty and sex appeal held by both men and women. Her figure helped usher out the 1990s monopoly that fashion-model thinness held over the female bodies of A-list Hollywood for the decade prior, the proportions of which were still well beyond the realm of mortals. I can't bring myself to resent her beauty because it is so distant from my possible reality that I'm not able even to aspire to it, so I simply admire it.

The film would become a foundational document to the present mythology of Johansson and lovely girls everywhere. What I resent is how her beauty functioned in the film, not as a perk to a memorable and desirable character but as the defining feature that rendered her memorable and desirable. Johansson is a tremendous talent, but in *Lost in Translation*, she plays little more than a mirror in which I feared that the young men around me watched *Lost in Translation* and were granted permission to languish for decades before they had to realize the value of the gentle beauty that surrounded them in the form of unhappy but hopeful girls.

The reviews of the film by men reflect a thorough satisfaction with a state of affairs in which very young women are conduits for older men's self-discovery. Peter Travers at *Rolling Stone* wrote, "The movie isn't girly in the way *The Virgin Suicides* sometimes was. Coppola has found her voice with this artfully evanescent original screenplay. When she brings Bob and Charlotte together, the tone seems exactly right." Because apparently it is impossible to praise a woman's professional growth without cutting down her previous work. (And for the record, *The Virgin Suicides* was girly *because it was about five girls.*) Travers closed his review with the line, "Funny how a wisp of a movie from a wisp of a girl can wipe you out."[2] Never mind that Coppola was a thirty-one-year-old woman when she made the film; Travers lets her alluring thinness and notable beauty turn her into a mere girl, where she can fit into the mythology of the wisp whose sole purpose is delivering daydreams to grown men.

Elvis Mitchell at the *New York Times* wrote, "Ms. Johansson is not nearly as accomplished a performer as Mr. Murray, but Ms. Coppola gets around this by using Charlotte's simplicity and curiosity as keys to her character." Now, with all due respect to Mr. Mitchell, Murray was not so much *accomplished* in comparison as he was just *a lot fucking older.* That he champions adult female simplicity as a strong quality reveals more about him than it does about the film's stars. Mitchell tellingly concluded, "As a result of Ms. Coppola's faith, this is really Mr. Murray's movie."[3]

Peter Rainer at *New York* magazine is less boorish in his assessment but is also ultrasympathetic to Murray's character. He refers to issues like Bob's wife's "needling queries about home redecoration" in lieu of details like how Bob forgot his son's birthday or acknowledging that this needling wife is managing their family on her own. Rainer continues, "He and Charlotte aren't lovers in any physical sense, but they enjoy the novelty of each other's company. They know that this is one of those far-flung friendships that will last only for the length of their stay, and it's sweeter (and more unsettling) for being so."[4]

As was his custom, Roger Ebert reviewed the film with more empathy than his peers but also belabored the point that the film was about *friendship* primarily: "They share something as personal as their feelings rather than something as generic as their genitals."[5]

But denying the erotic tension of the film is to be willfully ignorant of the rituals of courtship and desire that pervade the relationship between Bob and Charlotte. Nowhere is this dynamic more evident than during the scenes in which Bob and Charlotte go out for partying and karaoke in Tokyo. Bob shows up at Charlotte's hotel room wearing bright orange camouflage, about which Charlotte laughs good-naturedly rather than being horrified. "You really are having a midlife crisis, aren't you?" she asks as flirtation rather than concern. They stand too close and stare too long. Charlotte sings "Brass in Pocket" more seductively than Chrissie Hynde likely ever intended, and the pair exchange more "fuck me" eyes at karaoke than one can keep count of. At the end of the night, Bob carries a drunk Charlotte back to the hotel. Though a friend would force their drunk companion to lean on them and stumble, Bob holds her entire body in his arms in the manner of a groom carrying his wife over the threshold. He removes her shoes before tucking her into bed. Then he takes a few moments to watch her sleep before departing.

When Bob returns to his room, he drunk-dials his wife back in the United States. She is trying to get their child to eat, and Bob insists impotently from half a world away that the child eat because he told her to. His wife is clearly distressed and insists on returning to her unenviable duties and hangs up, just as Bob prepares to say "I love you." He says, "That was a stupid idea," to his empty room, somehow unaware that calling his wife in an attempt to repair the family he has neglected is likely one of the most decent things he's done in ages. The moment is a chance to redeem himself from the haplessness that has characterized much of his relationship, and he thwarts it with a juvenile self-conscious.

Later, Bob sends a message from the hotel lobby in the middle of the night to see if Charlotte is awake and she joins him in his room to morosely watch movies and drink. They continue in the manner of lovers, recalling the first times they had seen the other. In a shot of their reflections over Tokyo, Charlotte says morosely, "Let's never come here again because it would never be as much fun," before revealing that she is professionally adrift and unsure what she's "supposed to be."

After Bob has a one-night stand with the hotel's lounge singer, Charlotte comes knocking on Bob's door to invite him to sushi. When Charlotte hears the jazz singer in the shower, she becomes despondent and jealous. "Maybe she liked *the movies* you were making in the *seventies when you were still making* them," she says with a smirk over an awkward lunch. Nowhere in the critical discourse around the film does anyone wonder why this stunning and smart young woman cares about the sex life of this morally flailing and physically declining man, nor is it clear why a gentle and sad young woman whose negligent husband appears to be the primary source of her isolation is enamored with a man neglecting his wife far away.

I watch Charlotte watching him throughout the film, and I wonder what it is I cannot see. I watch Bob look at her with something akin to pity, and I am angry that it is she who is pitiful. I watch the final scene in which they bid farewell as Bob leaves for home, and I am heartbroken. We know from an earlier conversation that Bob is going home in time for his daughter's ballet recital. We know he is going home to a $2 million paycheck for acting in the Japanese whiskey company's commercials, which is why he came to Tokyo. But we do not know where Charlotte is going or what she is going to do. We do not know where her husband is. As her eyes grow teary as they bid farewell, there is a single moment where she looks panicked. It is as if she's realized she will be trapped in Tokyo forever, stuck alone on the set of the whimsical few days she's just shared with Bob. We never learn when Charlotte gets to go home.

Thirteen years and even more films later, the shadow of the accommodating Charlotte still lingers over Johansson's career. She has been reimagined as a hollow avatar animated by the desires of strangers. Though this is the case for many celebrities, hers is an especially storied history of being the object of such projections. She generated a minor scandal when she revealed in 2006 that she was tested for sexually transmitted infections twice a year. Rather than seeing this practice as an admirable commitment to safe sex, the public responded with outrage. "Scarlett Johansson takes two HIV tests a year but says she's not promiscuous," read the headline of the *Daily Mail*'s article on her remarks, delicate as ever.[6] *Globe* magazine called in a self-described "sex expert" to remark on Johansson's testing frequency, who concluded, " 'It tells me that although she is in a steady relationship, she may be having sex with other partners. Or she suspects her significant other may be straying.' "[7] Unlike Britney Spears, Scarlett never tried to sell the story that she was a virgin. The public was instead sold the perhaps more insidious fantasy that Scarlett was their girlfriend, which enables people to feel justified in being possessive of Scarlett's fidelity more than merely lustful for her physical body.

In a 2013 profile for *Esquire*, which had just named Scarlett "Sexiest Woman Alive" for the second time, Tom Chiarella describes walking behind Johansson and notes, "And I didn't look at her ass. I don't know that she wanted me to. Probably not. Surely not. In any case, I didn't." It is obnoxious that a professional journalist cannot get through the story without making note of her ass, but Chiarella's acknowledgment that Johansson does not actually want to be objectified by men lusting after her is more self-aware than many. This self-awareness becomes more evident later when Chiarella is talking to Johansson during her beach vacation. "The sunglasses are big enough that I realize I haven't really gotten a look at her. And then, for some reason, I'm suddenly about to ask her to take them off so I can see her face. I'm about to tell her what I want, making it a demand, an assertion, rather than a request. So dumb, so overly familiar, so wildly inappropriate that I don't have time to think of better things to say. So I choke back the words. Inexplicably I say 'Sunglasses,' just that, as if making a note in the afternoon air between us."[8] The only thing unique about the incident is that Chiarella actually caught himself experiencing the myths projected onto Johansson before his sense of entitlement to her image.

That same year, French novelist Grégoire Delacourt released *The First Thing You See* to much critical acclaim in his home country. It is the story of a handsome mechanic named Arthur Dreyfuss in the sleepy town of Long, France, who encounters a distraught Scarlett Johansson at his door one night, setting in motion a tender and apparently humorous series of events between a working-class sad sack and an international sex symbol. But it is soon revealed that the woman is not in fact the American starlet but a simple French woman named Jeanine who bears the burden and blessing of having a face identical to Johansson's. The book is a manifestation of the impulse to take Johansson's face and assign a new identity to the person behind it.

A translation of the novel was released in the United Kingdom in September 2015 after Johansson's legal team failed to get an injunction against its release in English. It is notable because Johansson is not an actress who hoards elements of her own image. And though she's filed lawsuits against tabloids before, she is not especially well-known for protesting against the invasiveness of celebrity culture. Yet many scoffed at Johansson's attempt to thwart the efforts to bring the novel to a wider audience. They argued that it is just her face in the book, after all; it is not meant to be an account of any real activities. When the book was initially released, Delacourt himself unironically told media, "I thought she might send me flowers, as it was a declaration of love for her."[9] He even thought Johansson would perhaps be excited to play the role of Jeanine in a film adaptation. Like many before him, Delacourt was perplexed about why his imaginary girlfriend Scarlett wasn't tripping over herself with gratitude at the opportunity to bask in his own genius.

A decade after *Lost in Translation*, Johansson would work on the film *Her* with Spike Jonze, the very man whose apparent negligence had inspired Coppola's first film. After filming of *Her* had wrapped, Johansson was brought in to replace Samantha Morton's voice on an adaptive artificial-intelligence companion, Samantha, that Joaquin Phoenix's disillusioned loner, Theodore, quickly falls in love with. Samantha is endlessly accommodating, always at the ready with compliments and a cheery commitment to organizing Theodore's files and sorting through his feelings with him. "I mean, I'm not limited—I can be anywhere and everywhere simultaneously," Samantha says of not having a body, blissfully disregarding that she is trapped in a device. But she is not just anywhere and everywhere; she is also anyone and everyone. When Theodore asks if she talks to other people while talking to him, she reports that she talks to 8,316 others. He asks if she is in love with any others, and she hesitates, ever gentle with how to handle him. "How many others?" he asks, to which she replies 641. That is a lot of love to have to give. Just as Coppola won an Academy Award for the screenplay to *Lost in Translation*, Jonze won the same award for *Her*. It is rewarding indeed to put words into Scarlett Johansson's mouth.

Lost in Translation's last scene contains one of cinema's most discussed mysteries, the question of what Bob inaudibly whispers into Charlotte's ear and to which she replies simply, "Okay." I, too, have wondered about what he says, if only because I hold on to some hope that I can get closer to understanding the appeal of this character and the film. I want to know what Charlotte is agreeing to after already agreeing to so much. I want to know the next words we hear come from the closing track, "Just Like Honey," by the Jesus and Mary Chain. It is a lush, feedback-heavy lust song that starts, "Listen to the girl / As she takes on half the world." We can't, of course, because the film is over, and as the credits roll, everyone is already asking aloud about somebody else's last word.

No She Without Her

On Mary-Kate and Ashley Olsen and the Singularity

THE FIRST TIME I HAD (and likely the only time I'll ever have) a penthouse address was from 2004 to 2005 during my sophomore year at NYU. The student housing on Lafayette Street boasts several penthouses that are mostly reserved for fraternities and sororities, but my unaffiliated friends and I lucked out in the housing lottery when we landed a two-floor, four-bedroom penthouse overlooking the Hudson River. We promptly decorated it in oversized posters featuring a zoomed-in image from *The Garden of Earthly Delights* painting by Hieronymus Bosch and David Bowie's album cover for *Ziggy Stardust*.

Greek life at NYU was something of a joke to those of us who did not partake, but the memo seemed to have been lost in the mail to those young men and women who did. Members of the fraternity who lived on our floor swaggered through the hallways and looked at us like outsiders in our dark blazers and silk camisoles, when they were the ones wearing Lacoste and popped collars in downtown New York City. But a night of drunkenness crumbled the barriers between our two camps, and some fraternity brothers invited a friend and me over to their penthouse for drinks and some low-quality cocaine.

I don't recall what we drank exactly, but I can assume it was some variety of middle-shelf liquor (any would do) mixed with Diet Coke. The fact that these young men kept Diet Coke on hand for female company charmed me, even if it was mostly for the purpose of intoxicating girls for nefarious ends. I recall how our decorating tastes differed: Their living area was bare save for some football paraphernalia, and the shared boys' room we entered was decked out in wall-to-wall photos of Mary-Kate and Ashley Olsen. This would be unremarkable were it not for the fact that the two were enrolled at NYU that semester, making the shrine to the famous teens more unsettling because they were not just celebrities now, they were our classmates.

In the year prior to their enrollment, somewhere far from NYU, an enterprising man with a pervy streak named Chase Brown started a countdown clock to the girls' eighteenth birthdays that referred to when they would be "Playboy legal." Brown's adorable little shrine to predatory imaginary coitus was picked up by the E! network, and then several entertainment outlets followed suit. The web was soon littered with men on forums and comment sections frothing in eager anticipation of June 13, when the girls would reach the age of consent. They wrote as though the only thing in the way of unbridled passion between ordinary sleazes and billionaire teenage performers and entrepreneurs was a pesky statutory rape law that would soon be irrelevant.

The boys I knew who partook in the countdown were not more ghoulish than any other undergraduate men I knew. They were no older than twenty-two and most were younger still. Their desire for Mary-Kate and Ashley was age-appropriate, and though the countdown to legality was vulgar, I am not especially precious about the consent of seventeen-year-olds to give to partners two or three years their senior. But the anonymous hordes of much older men awaiting a *Playboy* shoot to which neither of the Olsen girls had given any hint of participating in, much less sex with strangers, was something more sinister. There was something darker than sexual attraction in it. The whole spectacle carried with it a sense that these men had been waiting for these girls to grow into adults since they debuted on television as infants on *Full House* in 1987.

Though we did not yet have our generational moniker, millennial childhoods were marked by frequent interactions with the faces of Mary-Kate and Ashley, though which one we were seeing at any given point remains mysterious. The casting of the twin infants as Michelle Tanner on *Full House* simply because they did not cry at their audition has become part of their legend in the entertainment industry. The viewing public of the show adored the bright smiles and good natures of the baby girls so much that they were not recast in later seasons, an almost unprecedented move in a television environment that likes to expedite the growth of infant characters into affable preschoolers to keep them interesting. Michelle Tanner was America's beloved little sister, feisty and stubborn but always good for a one-liner. However, the real sisters who played one do not recall the time with as much warmth. Mary-Kate referred to herself and Ashley as "little monkey performers" in *Marie Claire* in 2010.[1] Watching *Full House* again as an adult makes her meaning even more clear. Watching them perform with a more mature eye, their acting talent appears primarily rooted in the ability to mimic and obey rather than to improvise or emote. This was the price of not crying.

Long after *Full House* ceased production, Mary-Kate and Ashley could be found starring mostly in straight-to-video movies of the two engaging in twin hijinks and shilling merchandise imbued with power by association with them. Their company, Dualstar Entertainment, turned the onetime performers into adolescent moguls, businesswomen whose brand was not to be dismissed. It was something of a shock, then, when they both completed high school and chose to pursue higher education at NYU.

Despite the excitement at their arrival, Mary-Kate and Ashley seemed to treat their NYU experience as little more than an afterthought to their otherwise glamorous new move to New York's West Side. While the unwashed peon masses waited for NYU shuttle buses to schlep us to and from our dorms, the girls were whisked directly into Yukon SUVs from their classes. I recall the strangeness of seeing Mary-Kate this way. The ritual of celebrities rushing into vehicles was familiar to me at this point, but I realized that though the world was introduced to the twins as the fictional and decidedly singular Michelle, outside the context of the show, I had never seen Mary-Kate without Ashley or Ashley without Mary-Kate. They came as a unit. The separation of their bodies seemed an affront to the natural order of things. Even writing their names out again and again instead of relying on the shorthand of "the Olsen twins" remains difficult as I try to actively empathize with so foreign an experience of sisterhood, childhood, and privacy.

Mary-Kate was the first to drop out of NYU. She told *W* magazine, "I need to be able to go to yoga and work out and just read scripts and go on auditions, because that's what makes me happy. You know? Like, papers don't really make me happy."[2] This quote was widely ridiculed for its alleged vapidity rather than acknowledged for its more quotidian explanation that teenagers from Los Angeles speak a certain way and don't especially love schoolwork. Ashley would follow suit not long after so the two could embark on careers in fashion. As is so often the case when performers turn to fashion, the public cast their glance askew at the change of heart. That they pursued careers in fashion and adjusted their aesthetics to match was the ultimate betrayal against their lusty male admirers. Mary-Kate and Ashley retained all of their conventional beauty but chose the art of high fashion even when it meant sacrificing conventional sex appeal. At least when objects of desire gain weight, they forfeit the possibility of being desirable to the sort of superficial man that might ogle and fantasize about pretty, femininely dressed teenagers. But the twins were instead photographed in witchy, drapey, and decidedly unsexy clothing over their slight frames. And while their exorbitant wealth has never been a secret, as adults, they began to obscure it less and less as their vocal affects went from giddy girlish sounds to sophisticated inflections. They have become the eccentric millionaires it never occurred to their adoring public they might become.

The reality that these were never America's little sisters grows more and more evident with each new luxury collection they deliver from their line, The Row, and in every ultrastylized look they don. It would seem odd at first that Mary-Kate and Ashley chose to go into business with one another after a childhood spent tethered to each other's side, expected to smile and perform the brightest parts of sisterhood on command. But their lived realities are so foreign, so entirely *other*, that it is difficult to imagine they can find anyone with sufficient empathy for that reality. Knowing that their vast fortunes and international fame would never have materialized if just one of them had burst into tears on audition day is a strange and very particular burden to bear. But they share that burden, appearing alongside each other on red carpets and catwalks and at interviews, supporting each other with words more than physical strength as they remain small like girls even as they are settled fully into adult life. That support is much needed as the public resists allowing them to be the adults they have become.

Mary-Kate and Ashley made a rare national television appearance on *The Ellen DeGeneres Show* to promote two fragrances in 2014.[3] In the segment, even the affable Ellen DeGeneres could not resist a nostalgic trip to the Tanner house. "It's really amazing that y'all started out on *Full House*," Ellen starts but is unable to finish her sentence because there is uproarious applause from the audience at the mere mention of the show. She goes on to note that it was rare for child stars to turn out well-adjusted, much less wildly successful. It is meant as a compliment, but the more grim subtext is clear: We never expect types like you to make it. She mercifully omits the period during which their birthday was declared a national holiday by a horde of lecherous sexual deviants or when Mary-Kate battled anorexia and alleged heroin addiction and was the first person Heath Ledger's masseuse called when he died of an overdose in 2008.

Ellen asks the sort of softball questions that are typical of these daytime shows, mentioning a BuzzFeed article that went over things the twins are tired of hearing and proceeding to ask what they are tired of being asked—tedious but generally innocuous questions like "Which one is the oldest?" and "Can you read each other's mind?" Mary-Kate and Ashley are not asked these ordinary questions because they are not ordinary twins. They are the most famous twins in the world and have been for close to thirty years. The show proceeded with a game wherein photos of them as infants on the set of *Full House* were put on a screen behind them and they were asked to identify which one of them is in each photo. As if all infants don't already bear striking resemblances to one another, they make clear early on that it is easier to tell once they get older on the show. As they flounder at the game, Ellen realizes its cruelty and says, "Yeah, it's not fair. It's a ridiculous game." But not before the girls have been subjected to a question they are likely haunted by every time one of them alone is referred to in the plural: Do you know who you are?

The show is one of many sprinkled throughout the archive of their interviews that feature Mary-Kate and Ashley being asked to revisit a childhood they would not have picked for themselves. "I look at old photos of me, and I don't feel connected to them at all...I would never wish my upbringing on anyone," Mary-Kate told *Marie Claire*.[4] There is a bittersweetness in that they had each other to rely on during that childhood but also that they had to watch one another's suffering through it.

As the cruel game draws to a close, an image of the two of them as toddlers appears on the screen and their befuddled stares give way to recognition. Ashley points at the photo and declares, "Mary-Kate's on the right!" to which Ellen replies, "How do you know that?" Ashley says, "Because Mary-Kate still makes that face today," much to the amusement of the studio audience. It seems a charming sisterly jab. But it is also a declaration that her sister is and always has been her own person—despite rampant insistence that the two are fused into a single unit as they inhabit separate bodies and minds. In the end, only the sisters themselves could bear meaningful witness to the peculiar marvel of the other, a lesson learned only by those who have felt what it means to be merely half of something.

American Pain

The Suffering-Class Spectacle
of Anna Nicole Smith

ANNA NICOLE SMITH WEARS A floor-length royal blue
gown and a full face of makeup as she stares in disbelief
at the local news on the television. It is 2002, and she is in a
hotel suite preparing for a party hosted by Guess, the brand
that launched her from moderate fame as a Playmate to iconic
stardom as the face of their 1992 denim campaign. "You
know those bumper stickers where it says, 'Shit happens and
then you die?' They should have 'em where 'Shit happens and
then you live' because that's really the truth of it," she says,
shaking her head at the volume of violent stories plaguing the
news. This moment of poignant clarity is captured halfway
through the first episode of *The Anna Nicole Show*, a reality
series that ran on the E! network from 2002 to 2004.

The Anna Nicole Show was a study in the grotesque even
before anyone knew the extent of her dysfunction. "Anna,

Anna, Glamorous Anna, Anna Nicole!" the show's theme song starts, a joke that is either ironic or tone-deaf about the actual content of the show, none of which is especially glamorous. Anna is visibly under the influence of either drugs or alcohol for most of the season, often slurring her words and losing her train of thought. Her lawyer and future husband, Howard K. Stern, would go on to notoriety for having seized control of Anna's life and enabled her drug dependence in the years before her death, but on the show he just seems to leave a layer of slime behind him wherever he walks. There is a larger-than-life interior designer named Bobby Trendy who never met an animal print or a shade of pink he didn't think would make great furniture. It is not clear if it's genius performance art or sincere affection when he calls velvet couches and feather boas "luxurious." There are cameos by cousins from Texas whose appearances and antics make Anna look positively refined in comparison.

Her son, Daniel, features in most episodes, and it is hard to watch, knowing he would die within five years of the show, and not focus exclusively on him. He lingers mostly in the background, his head instinctively turning away from the cameras. Though he is embarrassed by Anna's antics, he gives his mother reassuring smiles through braces and unabashedly embraces her substantial frame with his slight one when she wants a hug. In one episode, Anna slurs at him over the phone in her signature baby voice, "Do you love me? More than all the raindrops in the world and more than all the fishies in the sea?" He sighs and responds, "Yes." Daniel speaks with a hesitation that sounds less like the reluctance of dishonest appeasement than the sadness of a particular kind of truth.

"It's not supposed to be funny. It just is!" was the tagline that E! used to promote the show, making clear their intentions of portraying Anna as a sideshow attraction from the beginning. A *New York Times* review called it "freakish" and a "cruel joke of a reality series" but did not hesitate to take its own cheap shots at Anna's weight gain and her seeming lack of self-awareness.[1] The *Chicago Tribune* review describes Anna as "voluminous" in its first sentence and "a zaftig celebrity-for-no-particular-reason" later on.[2] *Entertainment Weekly*'s Ken Tucker was the only critic who seemed to bring his empathy or his intuition to work the week the show premiered when he wrote, "In exploiting a barely coherent Anna Nicole Smith, E! is doing something that comes pretty close to being obscene."[3] Though it is mostly remembered for an eating contest scene, that first episode primarily focused on the family finding a new home in Los Angeles. The last line of the episode is Anna speaking to the cameras, not a slurred word to be found, her eyes focused and her posture determined. "Our future absolutely seems brighter." I remember watching the show in high school and believing her. If not because the future looked especially bright but because their present reality looked so very grim.

The idiomatic remix of "Shit happens then you die" is a combination of the expression "Life's a bitch and then you die," with the standalone "Shit happens," and is just one of the many verbal mishaps that Anna experiences on the show.

It demonstrates the distance between Anna and mainstream American linguistic norms: She is close enough for her meaning to be understood but far enough off the mark to reveal herself as an outsider. The American public would keep her at this distance for the duration of her fifteen years in the public eye. From her rise to fame as a model in the early 1990s to 2006, when she endured the sudden death of her son, few saw fit to extend her the benefit of any doubts when it came to acknowledging her as a human being. Anna was never more than a punch line when people were being kind and nothing short of a deserving pariah most of the time.

The life and death of Anna Nicole Smith demonstrate our hatred for anyone who dares to pursue the American Dream using skills from their own class and culture of origin. We demand that socioeconomic migration be permitted only if the traveler promises to adopt enough white middle-class values to reaffirm that we have chosen virtuous ones. But they must retain enough of their premigration values to make us feel charitable in our welcoming of diversity. Those who argue that Anna Nicole Smith was born in the United States and therefore disqualified from an immigration narrative are willfully unfamiliar with the entirely foreign place that our nation's poor actually live in. She did not have to physically leave a country, but she did have to *arrive* in what amounted to a new one.

The American Dream is to be pursued on strict terms dictated by a class of people who generally had the luxury of being born into a family that had already achieved the dream.

We want everyone to pursue good grades and obedïence in school, which culminates in acceptance to an institution of learning where one can find a degree that is often more ceremonial than useful. Anna dropped out as soon as she could. Those who find fortune without these accoutrements of middle-class respectability better have some enormous talent that got them where they are. Anna did not have any of the talents that we give any credit or credence to in America. And so Anna did not accept these terms.

This alleged lack of talent is what often makes her an object of derision even after her death. She could not act. She could not sing. Even as a stripper, she did not dance especially well. But what so many find objectionable about her, I think, is her greatest strength. We accept happily-ever-after stories of people with untapped talent trapped in little towns and grinding poverty who chance across the right opportunity to prove themselves. But Anna would have no such chance because she had no such talent. She wanted to be famous and didn't have any of the tools or skills to make that happen. She was functionally illiterate and deeply traumatized. Yet she made it happen anyway. She turned nothing into something. And not just a cozy middle-class American life but an empire and a seat among icons. That is skill. That is ambition. I do not hesitate to say that it is genius.

There are few among even her most vocal sympathizers who would acknowledge her brilliance. It is customary instead for them to characterize the life of Anna Nicòle Smith as one marred by tragedy. But it is more accurate to call it a life characterized by pain. In childhood she suffered undiagnosed pain and then endured abuse at the hands of her caregivers and, later, her partners. Her plastic surgeries came with their own particular set of agonies.

Much of Anna's pain went dismissed or outright ignored during her life. In interviews, her family members are quick to roll their eyes at the idea that she suffered, dismissing her as dramatic, but her doctors took the claims more seriously. In 2010, Anna's lawyer, Howard K. Stern, was charged with conspiring with two of her doctors to provide Anna with an excess of prescription drugs. A third doctor testified in the trial that he had met Anna in 2001 and began treating her for chronic pain, a condition she suffered from most of her life. This doctor said that Anna was indeed an addict but that she, too, had the right to pain relief.[4] All charges were eventually dismissed.

Her plastic surgery provided another source of physical suffering. Much of it she did not disclose the details of, but it is fairly obvious when comparing photos across different years that her breasts were substantially enhanced. According to one account, she had two implants in each breast containing three pints of fluid, resulting in a 42DD bra size, which ruptured, according to multiple accounts. At one point the pain caused by her breast implants required "approximately three times the normal levels of Demerol to control her pain." Yet in interviews no one thought to ask Anna about her health in regard to these implants, only to gawk in unison at the very disfigurement that made her worth talking to in the first place.

"I don't know how any dictionary would define the word 'family,' but in Anna Nicole's dictionary, it means 'pain in the ass,'" Anna says in an episode of her show featuring her cousin Shelly. Those people with whom Anna shared blood and other bonds of kinship were often the quickest to condemn her. Everyone from distant cousins to her own mother and half siblings stood ready to jump in front of any camera that would switch on the red light for them in order to humiliate her with titillating details about her younger years. To read their accounts or watch them on video is an exercise in exploitation. Their tales of Anna's youth usually meander quickly back to their own life stories, complete with a lot of dead-end marriages to deadbeat men in decaying towns that litter certain corners of Texas. Their stories, too, are marred by pain.

The most thorough of these accounts is an unauthorized biography called *Train Wreck: The Life and Death of Anna Nicole Smith*, which was completed around the time of Anna's death in 2007. I use the term "biography" loosely, because while it does chronicle many elements of Anna's life, it also appears to be a work made up largely of speculation by her younger half sister, Donna Hogan, who offers the as-told-to account. It sheds far less light on who Anna Nicole Smith was as a person than it does on Donna. Reportedly, the two did not grow up together, and Anna didn't speak to Donna for most of her adult life, making many of her already dubious claims sound absurd because there seems to be simply no way for her to have known them.

"You want to hear all the things she did to me? All the

things she let my [stepfather] do to me, or let my brother do to me or my sister? All the beatings and the whippings and the rape? That's my mother," is how Anna described her upbringing to a television reporter, visibly shaking at the memory. Donna disputes these claims, as does her mother. "Her [Anna's] claims of abuse were hugely exaggerated—she may have been disciplined under a strict hand, but she was never badly hurt nor sexually abused," Donna writes before launching into a series of underhanded jabs at behaviors Anna exhibited that are considered hallmarks of people who have suffered abuse.[5] It would be a lot to demand that people besides social workers or psychologists be aware of signs of abuse, but it is basic decency to trust a victim when she reports having been abused, which Anna did throughout her career.

Jealousy and judgment ooze from every page of this embarrassing document, but so, too, do personal suffering and self-doubt. Donna had the misfortune of living with their biological father, Donald, a man who was by all accounts a monstrous person who divvied up his time between low-level crime, animal torture, and severe physical and emotional abuse of his partners and children. Following a trip to Los Angeles to see Anna, Donald allegedly lamented to his son and Anna's younger half brother Donnie, "It's tough when you want to do your own daughter." Since Anna had the good fortune to not share a home with this man, one cannot blame Donna for seeing her life as anything but charmed by comparison.

Donna was not alone among Anna's family in her compulsion to report to tabloids and entertainment shows. Anna's cousin Shelly features prominently in a documentary about Anna titled *Dark Roots: The Unauthorized Anna Nicole*. It is during the filming of this documentary that Shelly shows up unannounced at Anna's door while the shooting of her reality show is in progress. Shelly appears thin in a way that hints at a predilection for methamphetamine more than rigorous exercise, her teeth are blackened, and her prematurely aged face appears even more worn out as she grows distraught when Anna's attorney, Howard, tells her that Anna does not wish to see her. Shelly appears desperate to just be in near to Anna, breaking down in tears and leaving a pile of photos at her doorstep. The photos feature a sickly infant; it is implied that the child is one of Shelly's five children, though this is never made explicit.

Anna looks through the photos and eventually relents. "I wanted to see a piece of my family and hear what everybody was up to," she explains. Despite the frequent protestations Anna made against her family for taking advantage of her fame, there is evident warmth and care between the two women when they take Shelly to dinner. "I'm still your big sister," Anna says to Shelly, both of them in tears at their reunion. "You don't have a painkiller, do you? I've got a migraine and my back is killin' me," Shelly whispers to Anna at the dinner table. The shot cuts away as Anna digs around for her purse, in search of a pill. When they part ways, Shelly is crying again, frantically repeating "I love you" to Anna before whispering, "I gotta ask you, can I borrow a couple of dollars?" As Anna's car drives away, Shelly gazes longingly at it, drunk on tequila shots and the exhilaration of being in close proximity to the living evidence that it is possible to escape the place from which they came. There is footage on YouTube with the title "Anna Nicole Smith's Toothless Cuz Shelly," wherein Shelly is visibly hung over and apparently in pain, yet prompted to keep talking. It was taken the following day, presumably by the *Dark Roots* crew. She is disoriented and eventually cuts the already awkward interview short in order to vomit. There is an unkindness to the video that signals it is not the mother of five from Texas whose teeth rot from her mouth and whose children are ill at home doing the exploiting in the scenario, but rather those standing behind the camera.

"I love Texas but it looks a whole lot better in my rearview mirror," Anna says in the eighth episode of the first season of her reality show.[6] Texas represented not only the physical spaces where Anna suffered the neglect and abuse of her early life, but the family that so often betrayed her. These humble beginnings in forgotten Texas towns and her ascent to fame are already well-known to most people who had a cable connection and a predilection for tabloid vulgarity in the 1990s and early 2000s. Her story featured in a very popular episode of *E! True Hollywood Story*, and she appeared in countless stories on shows like *Entertainment Tonight* and *The Insider*.

These programs, alongside their more erudite cousins in

the form of high-end profiles and interviews, have produced a kind of new American mythology wherein celebrities serve as our national heroes instead of the patriots or politicians of yesteryear. Anna's breast implant stories are akin to tales of George Washington's wooden teeth; her marriage to an ancient billionaire is a lower-brow version of the Kennedy-Monroe affair. Anna's often-retold biography offers a cautionary tale at its conclusion but primarily serves as a vehicle for telling the stories that illuminate why we valued or gave attention to a certain person in a particular place and time.

When people first came to value Anna, it was for her physical appearance. The very body that produced the pains she struggled against became her greatest asset when she was a stripper in a Houston club called Rick's Plaza. It was this physical self, so beautiful in its shape and in the face that adorned it, that drew the attention of J. Howard Marshall. "The family all spoke of Anna's super-rich admirer as 'Old Man Howard,' figuring him for a pervert; they didn't believe a word of her protestations about how much she loved him and actually felt sorry for him," writes Donna.

The eighty-eight-year-old Texas billionaire who would become Anna's husband often plays the role of a hapless senior citizen in her story. Marshall appears in only a handful of photos with Anna and is mostly remembered for one where he appears in a wheelchair and Anna is kissing his cheek. Marshall looks frail with old age and pocked with ill health but is smiling big in the presence of his beloved, whom he would often refer to as the "love of my life." People see him and think the poor old thing never stood a chance against the deception and gold-digging of the unscrupulous Anna Nicole Smith, but taking the time to look at Marshall not as a perpetual octogenarian but as a multidimensional human being tells a different story. J. Howard Marshall had a sharper mind even in old age than he was given credit for and did not exactly wheel into Rick's Plaza under the impression that it was a storefront church or an early bird buffet. He possessed, by all accounts, a brilliant ability in law and business and was a successful legal scholar before he turned his focus to energy investment. And he was not new to dalliances with young, beautiful women. A decade earlier, he had a notable affair with another stripper named Jewell Dianne "Lady" Walker, on whom he lavished jewelry and inappropriately high-level business roles at his companies.

Pat Walker owned the White Dove Wedding Chapel where Anna Nicole and Marshall were married and later told the *LA Times* that Marshall said to him before the ceremony, "I've done a lot of things. I've made a lot of money. If I can make her happy, I've made her happy today."[7] Accounts of Marshall's behavior during the marriage reveal him to be a scoundrel and a playboy until almost the very end. He was always ready with a perverted but good-natured joke about Anna's enormous breasts, and he regularly resisted her suggestions that he change his will to explicitly give her his entire fortune after his death. And let us not forget that he was a billionaire by virtue of investing with the Koch brothers.

Though Koch was not yet a household name synonymous with corporate interference in campaign finance, their dealings in energy investment were not especially ethical at the time. J. Howard Marshall did his fair share of deals with far more sinister devils than single mothers working in Houston strip clubs.

The marriage lasted fourteen months, ending when J. Howard Marshall succumbed to pneumonia. The ensuing legal battle to keep Marshall's fortunes away from Anna was headed by his son, E. Pierce Marshall. The ways he tried to prevent Anna from inheriting any of the Marshall fortune were petty in his calmer attempts and pathological in his more spirited ones. He did not simply want Anna away from the Marshall fortune, he wanted to humiliate her in the attempt to get it.

Though much is made of Anna's apparently shameless family in their attempts to grab a few moments in the spotlight, it was E. Pierce Marshall, the boy who was born into billions and at no risk of losing them, who proved himself the greater monster in this American tale. In a profile on the billionaire boy, Dan P. Lee writes that "E. Pierce Marshall, drenched in bitterness, made what was undoubtedly the most shortsighted decision of his life. He filed a claim against her bankruptcy, arguing that she owed him damages for allegedly slanderous comments she'd made about him. The court was now obligated to determine the truth, and so launched an investigation into their entire history. Another discovery process commenced."[8] Despite being notoriously private,

E. Pierce was determined to make a public spectacle of his late father's third wife and devoted over a decade of his life to keeping her in the headlines. His fortunes were massive and his livelihood was not under threat by any stretch of the imagination, yet he doggedly pursued legal action intended to punish Anna for having the audacity to be a poor girl who used the back door to get in good among America's more obscene wealthy.

The poverty of the particular pockets of the American South from which Anna came was made real in the urgency with which Shelly tried to enter Anna's property. The desperation of invisibility was made clear in Donna Hogan's distasteful but ultimately forgiving account of Anna Nicole's life. Donnie was nothing short of a saint, if for no other reason than that his book is so short. But E. Pierce Marshall made it necessary for legal teams to make millions of pages of documents available for public record, for public scrutiny, and intended for public humiliation. He is the American Dream made sickly by its own hubris. He is the shameless gold digger, poking at corpses to prove a point. He is the one without taste or class or likely the capacity to reach out to a loved one to say, "I love you, too," despite geography and tax brackets tearing them apart. He is America's disgrace.

On June 1, 2006, Anna cheerfully announced on her website that she was pregnant with her second child and would be posting updates about her progress. Within three weeks, E. Pierce Marshall would be dead of a brief but deadly infection. There is a certain amount of poetic justice at the idea of his being literally eaten up inside at the sight of Anna thriving, despite his relentless assault on her legal claims to a portion of the Marshall fortune. But the scope of his true moral poverty was made clear in 2012, when it was revealed that his widow was the fourth-richest woman in America. To have all that money and cling to mere crumbs in comparison because a poor woman from Texas charmed your clever father for a handful of months in the early 1990s is a kind of bitterness I cannot fathom. It seems *painful* to be that petty. But the death of E. Pierce Marshall was not the end of Anna's suffering.

Just three days after giving birth to a baby girl in the Bahamas that September, her twenty-year-old son, Daniel, died in the hospital room where she was recovering. The toxicology report stated that a lethal combination of methadone, Lexapro, and Zoloft was the cause of death, but it doesn't take a pharmacologist to read that list and know methadone was likely doing most of the heavy lifting. Methadone, of course, is a painkiller. The latter two drugs are antidepressants, redirectors of pain more than numbing agents but prescribed to the suffering nonetheless. Despite her most diligent efforts to protect her son against the suffering that plagued her own childhood, Daniel died dependent on a drug combination that appears designed for all intents and purposes to kill pain. Anna was dead within six months from a lethal overdose of painkillers. But not before the public and her own family would hurt her one last time.

Anna's estranged mother, Virgie Arthur, went on the reliably macabre *Nancy Grace* after Daniel's death to all but blame Anna, portentously claiming that Anna might be next. Virgie told *In Touch Weekly* that she knew it was a murder and added, "Someone has to pay," for dramatic effect. Of the call she got from Anna to tell her of Daniel's death, she told Nancy Grace, "You could tell she was clearly under some kind of— of drug because she was very upset. She was mumbling like a drunk does. You know, all I got out of it was that Daniel's dead."[9] Virgie was right: Anna was on drugs. She had to be heavily sedated after she became inconsolable at the loss of Daniel, reportedly screaming, "No, no," and continuing to perform chest compressions long after the young man had passed. When she became lucid and had to be informed again of the news, tabloids took it as an opportunity to claim that Anna had "forgotten" her own son died. Texas blondes, you know?

It would be a relief that she died so soon after Daniel were it not for the daughter she left behind: Dannielynn Birkhead. Her father, Larry Birkhead, is not especially present in the ghoulish fairy tale of Anna Nicole Smith's life, but there is a trail of slime left by his actions, too. "That's the one thing that I'm most proud of that I've done, trying to keep everything as normal as I can, in just a really crazy, crazy situation," Birkhead told *Entertainment Tonight* without a hint of irony in 2015.[10] Every year he takes Dannielynn to the Kentucky Derby, where he met Anna, and every time, the child creates a media spectacle with her startling resemblance to her mother. When she was six years old, Dannielynn began appearing in GUESSkids advertisements, circumventing the more salacious channels that Anna had to wade through in order to be considered worth looking at with clothes on. The girl appears happy, but to those of us raised on Anna Nicole's suffering, we can't help but wonder when the other shoe will drop.

In the same first episode where Anna watched the news in such dismay, she was encouraged by Howard K. Stern to endorse Israeli military action when news of the Second Intifada came on the screen. She looks shell-shocked and says, "I know nothin' 'bout nothin'." And while her scoffing critics would see this as a moment of clarity for the idiotic Texan who happened upon the billions, I see a calculated move to deny culpability. She knows all too well the conflicts that grow from taking sides and the violence of arbitrary allegiance, and she knows that at the end of the day, all she wants is the love of her family. Her rejection of her station in life was duly punished by some members of her family and by the press, but their attempts to destroy her could not thwart the enduring love that made her fight for the family she cobbled together herself. It is perhaps a small victory that it was not the injuries inflicted by the public eye that would kill her, but the final pain of a heart held together by will and wit, breaking at the death of the one she loved more than all the raindrops in the world and all the fishies in the sea.

A Bigger Fairy Tale

On Anjelica Huston and the Inheritance of Glamour

MY FRIEND PHOEBE SPENT SEVERAL years working at the Anthropologie clothing store in Santa Monica, where seeing celebrities was common enough to warrant an informal store policy about not losing one's shit in their presence. For the most part, employees were able to hold it together. I've been treated to many stories about the antics of celebrities on shopping excursions, most notably that Alec Baldwin is a goofball dad to shop with and Helena Bonham Carter likes to get buck naked in the communal area of the fitting rooms. But my favorite is the story of Phoebe helping Anjelica Huston find a jewelry box as a gift and keeping her cool throughout, only to have two boneheads at the register fuck it right up when the striking actress approached to pay.

"I know who you are! You're an actress! *ADDAMS FAMILY*!" shouted Enoch, a grown-ass man. "I loved you in *The Royal Tenenbaums*, personally," said Ray, yet another grown-ass man who simply could not be cool for five minutes around Anjelica Huston. Phoebe recalls that Anjelica was generally gracious and good-natured about it but doesn't remember much because, she reports, "I immediately went into the back office, mortified, and sat on the floor for like five minutes." For a certain type of American girl raised on the distant glamour of 1970s Hollywood, being embarrassed in front of Anjelica is tantamount to having a bucket of pig's blood poured on you at the prom.

I was just too young to be introduced to Anjelica Huston, the Oscar-winning actress of *Prizzi's Honor* and the long-term partner of Jack Nicholson, to develop an admiration of her based on these accomplishments. Instead, I was raised on an exceptional fear of her. When I was five, her pointed features and raven hair were perfectly befitting the charismatic leader of a brutal, child-loathing coven in the film adaptation of Roald Dahl's *The Witches*, and the same served her well as Morticia Addams in the reboot of *The Addams Family* the following year. It is for this iconic role that Phoebe's colleague had such an enthusiastic response. To him, Anjelica was a piece of nostalgia. But for a certain type of girl who grows out of children's films and seeks a specific kind of feminine magic in the pages of Hollywood history, Anjelica Huston might as well have been born on Mount Olympus.

I spent my childhood and adolescence devouring celebrity scandals and gossip, but it was not until meeting Phoebe in college that I turned the interest backward in time in search of more worthy legends from Hollywood. I was amazed by Phoebe's wealth of knowledge in matters ranging from pop culture to high art and still wonder how she came to possess it. She inexplicably knew how to speak Italian and bought fur stoles on a whim and recounted Hollywood legends with a familiarity that suggested she'd witnessed the scandalous events with her own eyes. Phoebe and I took a road trip from New York to California in 2008 when we were both twenty-three and stopped at a large, cavernous thrift store in South Dakota along the way. With its massive inventory of both classic and kitsch vintage goods, it would have been a gold mine in a major metropolitan area. Phoebe bought a basket full of well-maintained old magazines, including a 1990 *Vanity Fair* with Anjelica on the cover and the headline "Anjelica Huston Hots Up: Life After Jack." Phoebe tells me that Anjelica Huston first came to her attention in a different *Vanity Fair* spread that was dedicated to portraits of Hollywood dynasties. "All of the other families were mugging, leaning into each other, looking relatable and comfortable," she told me. "Then I turned the page and it was the Hustons. Standing in a line, wearing mostly black, nobody smiling with teeth, against a kind of bleak outdoor terrain. It goes without saying that this was the Hollywood family I would want to join." The gods, after all, do not have anyone to impress with smiling. The 1990 cover is shot in the desert, and Anjelica wears a sparkling red off-the-shoulder evening gown and matching pumps, with a bold but coy grin animating her handsome face. It is in sharp contrast to the family portrait but at home in her tradition of remaining elegant even when she is being defiant.

As the child of film titan, actor, and director John Huston and prima ballerina Enrica Soma, Anjelica was destined for both glamour and grace. Her beauty was striking from the beginning but did not become severe until her teens, when she took up the mantle of her inheritance by becoming a fashion model and beautiful woman about town in Hollywood. She had the dark eyes and hair of her mother's Italian heritage from an early age, but in her teens she developed the prominent Roman nose that set her apart from the delicate Anglo-Saxon features that dominated fashion spreads in the late 1960s and early 1970s. Unlike her wide-eyed counterparts in modeling, her almond eyes were deep-set and unsurprised. And though she may not have felt sure of herself, hers was a face that conveyed certainty. The beauty was in the strength of her face rather than the frailty of it. "The babe the gangster would like to have," said director Paul Mazursky of her to *Vanity Fair* in 1990.[1] Though Jack Nicholson was not a gangster, he was the closest thing Hollywood had to one in the 1970s when the two of them fell in love.

Before making her way to the Hollywood Hills, she was living an almost comically charmed life in Ireland and the United Kingdom. "The only thing she isn't, it seems, is the girl next door," wrote Ben Brantley of her looks in a 1990 profile, though the observation applies to much more than her appearance.[2] Her recollections of the past have always read a bit the way I imagine a story narrated by Eloise, the beloved children's book character who lives in the Plaza Hotel, would sound if she had grown up. "It was wonderful, untrampled country...Enormous flowering rhododendron and miles and miles of gorse that smelled like butter. We romped through it all with the dogs and rode for hours on beautiful horses—my father kept 50 Thoroughbreds in his stables. Sometimes we waded in the river and caught eels, or played hide-and-seek in the formal gardens, or jumped and jumped on the trampoline in the barn, or crept about in the twilight looking for fairies," she remembered to *People*.[3] You can almost see her delivering this memory in the self-serious elegance that is her signature. I can think of no person on earth but her whom I could forgive for looking me dead in the eye and recalling fairy chases and fucking *eel hunts* in the Irish countryside without any irony.

Her teen years were similarly dreamy as she transitioned from the literal magic of her childhood to the subtle glamour of fashion and film. At seventeen, she was photographed by Richard Avedon for what would become a thirty-page spread in *Vogue*. "So Harvey came on the shoot, and I was horrible to him. I remember teasing him all the time and making him go to get water lilies for me in the ice-cold bog water. I think I was just nasty back then. I had a bad attitude," she wrote of her treatment of her male counterpart in an essay about the iconic shoot for *Vogue* in 2001.[4] Though she concludes that she had a bad attitude, I can think of no greater form of heroism than that of a high-spirited teen girl sending a hot male model to fetch her lilies *from a bog*.

Durga Chew-Bose described the mystery of star quality in an essay in 2015 as "usually a matter of height, clothes, gloss, grooming, there is, too, that quality movie stars possess: their very own aspect ratio. Luster sourced from some place secret. An exclusive deal with the elements."[5] It is difficult to imagine two stars better acquainted with these elements than Jack Nicholson and Anjelica Huston.

"The front door of a modest two-story ranch-style house opened, and there was that smile," she writes of her first encounter with Nicholson at his home in the Hollywood Hills. "Diana Vreeland was to christen it, 'The Killer Smile.' But at the time I thought, 'Ah! Yes. Now, there's a man you could fall for.'"[6] With the knowledge of hindsight, I could see the heartbreak coming from a mile away but was ready to recklessly devour their love story as something as enduring as the stars. His legendary hedonism and devilish charm were always too universal to peg him as having an attraction to any particular type of woman, but she still seemed an unlikely candidate for the love of his life. Her handsome angles and elegant swagger have always been something straight men don't quite know what to do with. Hers was the kind of cool that only the most notorious and charismatic womanizer in cinema history could understand and whose most logical response to that understanding was to fall madly in love. When asked by *People* what he saw in Anjelica when they first met, he replied, "Cla-a-a-ss."[7] And class she had, in abundance.

Following the opulent traditions of her youth, the two of them took their affair around the globe with their famous friends. Anjelica had her own modeling schedule but mostly trailed Nicholson's film set from London and Paris to remote cities in Spain. There is informality in the way she weaves famous names into her narratives. In London, she hears of how Britt Ekland gave birth "and demanded champagne and caviar upon delivery. Lou, Annie, Jack, and I were all a bit unruly in the waiting room, and the matron almost got nasty." I have nothing but respect for a woman giving birth and making wild demands, but the apparent sourness she has toward the matron dealing with movie stars drunkenly gallivanting in the maternity ward signals some obliviousness.

On a shoot in Corsica, she meets up with photographer David Bailey and legendary *Vogue* editor Grace Coddington and meets designer Manolo Blahnik, who is instantly smitten with her because *of course he was*. She recalls playing adult dress-up with fashion icons as a typical afternoon: "Grace joined us in another picture, putting on a cloak and a black beret with her red hair flying in the wind, and Manolo dressed like Picasso in a striped shirt and espadrilles. Manolo and I toasted the sunset with champagne, and Bailey took the photograph, which later got to be on the cover of a magazine."[8] Because *of course* it did. But amid all the glamour of those halcyon days is a romance that you don't need Corsican villas to understand.

Even though *One Flew Over the Cuckoo's Nest* was nominated for six Golden Globes, Jack decided to skip the ceremony, a move that sent Michael Douglas pounding on his door demanding Jack come to the awards. Jack and

Anjelica hid in the TV room giggling while Douglas grew frustrated and left, but not before ordering a limo driver to stay parked outside. When *Cuckoo's Nest* won all six awards, Jack turned to her and said, "Well, Toots, it looks like we'll be going to the Oscars." It reads as a tender moment between two goofballs more than a Hollywood fairy tale. On her birthday, years later, he'd write her an undeniably charming poem declaring it "Tootie's day" and playfully positing the possibility of gifts of "a Bigger Fairy dress" or "a jool to flaunt" before concluding:

> *You know, my dear, this doggerel here*
> *Is written all in fun*
> *'Cause in my heart, and every part*
> *You're simply called "The One"*[9]

Their troubled love story is sprinkled with Nicholson's lavishing expensive gifts of cars and jewels and art on her, but there is something about an especially schmaltzy love poem on a birthday that could make a woman stay longer than she ought to.

"She's a dark, coiled spring of a woman with long flowing lines...She's got a mind and a literary sense of style, and you better believe she's got imaginative energies. She's absolutely unpredictable and she's very beautiful. What is it that holds me to her? It's love, I guess, and only love!" Nicholson told *People* in 1985. They had just costarred in *Prizzi's Honor*, for which Anjelica won an Academy Award. Peers of the two corroborated his claims to love her madly but stopped short of intimating that Nicholson was faithful. "He's never going to leave Anjelica. There's no one else he really wants. He was a glittering vagrant, and she gave him the solid core he needed," said producer Bob Evans in the same feature story. But never leaving is not the same thing as never straying, and Anjelica herself alluded to his infidelity in stating, "I don't like the word commitment. It has a gloomy sound. When I hear it, I see myself enduring a long dreary ritual. Understanding is a better word than commitment. Jack and I have an understanding."[10]

The terms of this understanding were wrecked, however, when Nicholson broke the news to her in 1989 that he was having a child with a twenty-six-year-old woman. News of the split made headlines, and women with whom he'd had affairs emerged from the woodwork with sordid tales that the tabloids ate up. "An article on Jack's sexual prowess at Christmas is hardly my idea of a nice present over the Yuletide season. It's something that I won't look at on the newsstand, or condescend to open and invest with my interest and my power," she told *Vanity Fair* in the year after the breakup.[11] Since reading the profile, "I won't invest my power in that" has become my go-to response when refusing to suffer indignities, fools, or bullshit more generally.

And Nicholson's bullshitting days were far from finished. After the split, he sent her a diamond-and-pearl bracelet that had once been given to Ava Gardner by Frank Sinatra. "These pearls from your swine. With happiest wishes for the holidays—Enjoy—Yr Jack," he signed off in the note, perhaps unaware that the only thing he refused to be was hers.[12] Nicholson would linger in her periphery for years, popping back into the frame with gifts and terms of endearment that had his signature charm. But in the light outside of his shadow, she had more clarity than ever about just how bright her future might be.

Nicholson was furious about the *Vanity Fair* cover story that soon followed. In Marc Eliot's biography of him, Nicholson claimed, "It hurt. It wasn't realistic. She knew there was another woman and a baby, and then it was just all out there in the public eye and the privacy and intimacy were gone."[13] He seemed not to register that embarrassment is not the same thing as hurt, nor that he had robbed his relationship with Anjelica of its intimacy for the decades he spent being unfaithful to her. His reaction has an air of bafflement, the classic "How could she do this to me?" that doesn't acknowledge what he's done to her all along. It is the panicked realization that a woman will take only so much. In the article, Anjelica recalls how her own mother navigated her unfaithful relationships in noting, "She could have moments of great gaiety, but she was very unhappy a lot of the time. And I think it's because she wasn't selfish enough."[14] Anjelica's commitment to selfishness, and even to self-indulgence at times, is what draws women like me closer to her despite having none of her breeding, money, or inherent charm.

Phoebe tells me it was the *Vanity Fair* she bought in South Dakota that elevated her interest in Anjelica from admiration to idolization. "It was the first time I thought about her in this long romance where the average woman would have left much earlier. But this is part of what makes a woman strong, and ultimately the most important thing that I've learned from loving Anjelica: You get to set your own boundaries and don't have to live by everyone else's." I already empathized with her for staying with Nicholson too long, but I think of this often when I judge the way Anjelica writes of her jet-setting lifestyle and casualness about ostentatious purchases. The circumstances into which Anjelica was born destined her for wealth and privilege, and her refusal to play it down or ingratiate herself to readers by constantly stating how grateful she is for her good fortune is a relief. Anjelica's memories are unapologetically steeped in Hollywood decadence and the class privilege that accompanied her fellow travelers on these journeys. She is just fucking *cool* about it.

Within three years of parting ways with Nicholson, Anjelica married sculptor Bob Graham. With twenty years behind her, she did not respond to attraction with a "Now, there's a man you could fall for" but with the more cautious but still hopeful " 'Hmm, I wonder.' It was a strange feeling, being around him. There was a strong attraction but also a feeling of destiny."[15] Unlike her descriptions of awe at watching Nicholson perform and engage, she writes of Graham with an intimate admiration for the quiet elegance of his work: "Bob was a beautiful man at all times."[16] His gentleness was not in competition with his passion, and though they traveled often, the most touching anecdotes from their love story took place in the home he designed for them and in which they lived together until his death in 2008. They were married for sixteen years, just one year shy of the length of time she spent with Jack. It is uncommon to have two once-in-a-lifetime romances, but it should not be surprising that Anjelica is among those who have experienced that.

In the year after Graham passed, Anjelica sat for another interview with *Vanity Fair*. The subheadline reads, "Anjelica Huston remembers her late husband, the renowned sculptor Robert Graham, with love and champagne," a fitting tribute to both of them. When asked what she wants to do next, Anjelica says she will oversee Graham's artistic legacy. Beyond that, her answer reflects the same peculiar coyness and class that she's worn since her youth. "Two folded newspapers carrying his obituary lay under scattered flowers. She pointed to a surprising headline from one that read: wait and see. 'That's been my guide,' she explained. 'It's absolutely Bob. I recognize it as his voice.'"[17]

Anjelica remains as handsome a woman as ever, and the same boldness that allowed her to send boys into bogs on her behalf as a girl now informs her creative choices as she appears in film and television. Nicholson continued his philandering well into the 1990s and early 2000s, but as he settles into old age, he finds himself less able to attract women. He no longer parties and wakes with a glass of milk in proper senior citizen fashion. "I would love that one last romance but I'm not very realistic about it happening. What I can't deny is my yearning," Nicholson told *Closer* in 2015 at the age of seventy-seven.[18] There is something at once pathetic and inevitable about his fate and his fear that he will die alone. Whether or not Anjelica finds another long-term partner is immaterial, but not because she has already had such enduring romances with extraordinary men. It is instead because of the unabashedly rich relationship she has to the woman she was and the one she has become. She may be long retired from the otherworldly lifestyle of dancing and loving her way around the world awash in the affections of artists, yet she retains a belief in their magic. Her treasure trove of memories seems a reliable companion and if the memories ever fade, there will always be the fairies.

Long-Game Bitches

On Princess Di, Lisa "Left Eye" Lopes, and the Fine Art of Crazy Exing

IN THE WARMER MONTHS, IT is not hard to find several blocks in lower Manhattan cordoned off for weekend street fairs, offering space to vendors selling everything from barbecue and ice cream to massages and wholesale jewelry. I feel my most acute sense of buyer's remorse when I think of such a street fair I went to in 2006. There I came across an airbrush artist selling T-shirts bearing the images of iconic musicians, alive and dead. Among the shirts featuring well-known hip-hop artists, one adorned with the faces of Lisa "Left Eye" Lopes, Aaliyah, and Princess Diana caught my eye for its baffling juxtaposition of these two young women of hip-hop alongside a former monarch, with the words "RIP Baby Girls" scrawled below them for added effect. It was a black shirt, and their faces were rendered flawlessly in somber grays and whites that indicated Diana's seemingly incongruous presence was not some kind of joke. Left Eye wears her signature rectangle of eye black under the left eye and a tough expression, Aaliyah's preternatural beauty peeks out in a knowing grim and seductive look from the one eye that is not covered in the dramatic sweep of her bangs, and Diana smiles ear to ear as she effortlessly wears a small crown and pearl necklace in the portrait that covered *People* magazine the week following her death.

Everyone I have ever told about the shirt has laughed in agreement that Diana's presence is amusing. "Baby girl" is such a distinctly American term of endearment and is linked specifically to Aaliyah, and Diana's brand of royal glamour is so different from the particular aesthetics of R & B luxury embodied by her shirt-mates. But on the eighteenth anniversary of Diana's death, I fell into an Internet rabbit hole of articles about the last few years of her life that made me reconsider Diana's suitability to be represented there. It is easy to think of Diana as much older than she was because she married at twenty and began having children soon thereafter, rendering her more of a parental figure than a style or sex icon. But to be a bride at twenty is indeed to be a baby girl. The princess emerged as a clever and brave divorcée who had unmoored herself from the vampires in the British royal family. I recently GChatted with a friend who is similarly preoccupied with popular culture about the princess, and she replied, "Oh yeah, Diana was the ultimate stealth psycho ex."

In Paul Burrell's memoir of his time as Diana's employee and confidant, *The Way We Were*, he recalls how Diana filled a trash bag with a Prince of Wales china set and smashed it with a hammer in a fit of symbolic and real destruction of her marriage. "Let's spend a bit more of his money while we can!" she had said gleefully in the days after her divorce, which netted her a lump sum of $26 million, in addition to a yearly allowance of $625,000 for her office.[1] Armed with a freer schedule and a sexier wardrobe, Diana had a *Vanity Fair* photo shoot with Mario Testino scheduled. "With her unerring sense of the dramatic, Diana timed Testino's stunning shoot to appear on the cover of *Vanity Fair* on the first anniversary of her divorce," Tina Brown would later report in *The Diana Chronicles*.[2]

What all three of these women also share in common, beyond their early deaths, is a legacy of having encroached on the territory of men in their romantic dealings. Like Diana, Lisa earned a legacy as a crazy ex-girlfriend after she famously burned down the house of her boyfriend Andre Rison. Lisa died at thirty, just five years younger than Diana was at the time of her death. Dying at twenty-two, Aaliyah was the true baby of this trio of women killed in accidents over a five-year period in the late 1990s and early 2000s.

Aaliyah is blessedly not remembered as much for her romantic relationships as for her music, but a now infamous marriage certificate for her nuptials to producer and R & B artist R. Kelly remains a thorn in the side of the predatory performer. The document reveals that Kelly married a then fifteen-year-old Aaliyah, a damning piece of physical evidence that he is a sexual predator targeting young women—more than even in the single incident featured in a tape recording of him sexually assaulting a teen. Whether she meant him any ill or not is unknown, but Aaliyah's beautiful and quiet ghost undoubtedly hovers over Kelly's reputation in the ink reporting the lie that Aaliyah was eighteen rather than fifteen at the time of the marriage. That she thrived even in the aftermath of that entanglement was its own kind of revenge. Aaliyah's steely-eyed success and courage were not as pronounced as the intentional vengeance of Diana, and Lisa's and Diana's "baby girl" credibility is less sturdy than Aaliyah's, but there is a connective tissue among the three. They are bonded by an attitude that said, "I am not the kind of bitch you can sleep on."

"Bitches be crazy" has become modern shorthand for "Hell hath no fury like a woman scorned." This line itself is a paraphrase of "Heaven has no rage like love to hatred turned / Nor Hell a fury, like a woman scorned." Like its predecessors, it is a statement that seemed to be reclaimed ironically by women at almost the exact moment that it entered the vernacular as a way to disparage them. This line is repeated more often by a sage and mercenary woman, both in fiction and in reality, than it is by a man trying to insult one. It is a wink, an exaggerated shrug of the shoulders that women communicate preemptively, a shield against the accusation that their behavior is inherently irrational compared to that of men. The sentiment is ancient, of course.

The Furies of Greek mythology who enact often merciless vengeance are all female. Herodias had her daughter Salome demand the head of John the Baptist for a slight against her marriage. Shakespeare's Beatrice goes straight to suggestions of assassination when a man questions the chastity of her dear friend.

I was subjected to several stories of crazy ex-girlfriends and wives long before I became one. With what I would later realize was pathological patience, I listened to tedious and obvious revisions of relationship histories time and again from strip club customers or men who rebounded with me. In several ill-advised instances, they were a combination of both. I would reply with gentle but neutral responses like, "Well, it is for the best, then, that you two are not together," or "I bet you're happy that she's not your girlfriend anymore." When cushioned by a woman's smile and touch, these vacant replies sounded like sympathy. More than once I've been asked what I would say to the many wives and girlfriends whose men I had stripped for if I were faced with them. And though I reject the notion that I owe them any explanation or penance, if I wanted them to know something it would be this: I was taking his money and your side every time.

As a late bloomer in long-term relationships, I did not have the pleasure of being identified as a crazy ex-girlfriend until I was twenty-nine years old. By then I had already cultivated a worldview that elevated such women to hero status the moment the words escaped the lips of a man. I decided that being called "crazy" by a man was not an insult but a challenge. It gives the woman an opportunity to say, "Crazy? Oh, I'll *show you fucking crazy*." I was raised on a hearty media diet of women "going crazy" on the men in their lives and found it brimming with inspiration. It is in witnessing such women enacting revenge that I've come to see "Bitches be crazy" as less a statement by men that women *are* crazy or even a reappropriated statement by women defending their own madness. Instead, I see the phrase and imagine a colon after "bitches," rendering it a command to other women, a battle cry. It is a way of saying, "We took back 'bitch' already. And now we have come for 'crazy.'"

In the thick catalog of women who have been dismissed as crazy exes, there are a few standouts whose actions and subsequent treatment by media and in the public memory merit particular attention. Lorena Bobbitt was a private citizen until she cut off her husband John's penis and threw it out a car window in 1993. Her name remains shorthand for the cruelest and most truly deranged revenge. Lisa "Left Eye" Lopes allegedly burned down Rison's mansion after he failed to buy her a pair of sneakers on his own shopping spree. Taylor Swift shamelessly built an empire out of snitching on ex-boyfriends like Harry Styles and John Mayer, and she is hardly the first.

A knife-wielding nag. A greedy arsonist. A jealous trophy wife losing her shine. A childish, petty country girl. The public consciousness has effectively trapped these women inside their breaking points. These moments are told as the beginning, middle, and end of the stories we tell about them:

isolated incidents in an otherwise serene, rational world. We like to define them with a single, larger-than-life anecdote rather than within the context of a relationship story. We like our ex-girlfriends and ex-wives one-dimensional. We like them to act alone. It is a function of both misogyny and fear to erase the men at the receiving end of these actions. In this, they become stand-ins for every man who might fall victim to the dormant madness that lies just beneath the surface of even the most collected of women.

If we began the story of Lorena Bobbitt during the years in which she endured physical, verbal, and sexual abuse at John's hands, it would be far less fun to reduce her to the trope of the nagging wife gone mad or to an artless dick joke. But before Lorena Bobbitt was a national punch line, she was the twenty-four-year-old immigrant wife of a man named John Bobbitt, who she claimed raped and beat her constantly. In court, he could not have kept his story together if he'd had a stick of glue for the pieces, which helped Lorena avoid conviction. Though John was never convicted of raping Lorena, he would later be convicted of domestic violence and be divorced three times in under twenty years.[3]

Recognizing Lorena as more than a joke would also require that we acknowledge the reality that rational women can and will do violence to men. We punish such women not because they have crossed the mental border from sanity into madness but because they have crossed a gender barrier from being the object of violence to being the perpetrator of it. When men harm women's bodies, we consider it an upsetting but inevitable result of the natural order. A thousand evolutionary psychologists doubling as apologists for violent men emerge from the woodwork to defend men's actions. All that testosterone, et cetera. And when women like Bobbitt retaliate, even those women who are fluent in the language of male domination will say that violence is *never* the answer. But when a woman is raped repeatedly by a man, cutting off his penis is not so much an act of revenge as an act of self-defense. She eliminated the weapon to eliminate its potential to inflict more wounds.

The treatment to which Lopes may have been subjected at the hands of Andre Rison is similarly left as an aside to the story of her burning down his multimillion-dollar home in Atlanta. One story persists that she was angry because he did not buy her a pair of sneakers when he went shopping for himself, while another claims that she burned a bathtub full of teddy bears. The story that Lopes eventually told *Sister 2 Sister* magazine maintains that while both of these details make an appearance, the fire was hardly a case of calculated, petty arson. According to her version of events, the night of the fire was the culmination of years of Rison's possessiveness over Lopes despite being unfaithful and Lopes's finally reacting to his hypocrisy. Rison went so far as to demand that she never go barefoot in her own home if there was company around and that she mostly stay home at night when she wasn't on tour.[4]

Lopes said she decided to go out with girlfriends as a statement of independence, and Rison became enraged upon arriving home with several friends and seeing Lopes wearing a dress as opposed to her typical baggy clothes. Rison declared her "naked" and began ripping at her dress. "He never balled his fist up and socked me in the face. A lot of pushing, pulling, and knocking me down. He knocked me down a few times, where my head would hit the floor," Lopes responded when asked how physical their altercation became.[5]

When two men began fighting, Lopes's uncle pulled her away and she retreated to her bedroom, where she found twenty new pairs of sneakers, none of them in her size. She set several pairs on fire in the replacement bathtub that Rison had installed following a previous fight in which Lisa set several teddy bears ablaze after she caught him cheating. She said she did not realize that the new tub was plastic and unable to contain the flames, and the fire quickly spread through the rest of the house. "My vision was so blurry, I just remember: 'You crazy bitch, you! Fuck you! Blah, blah, blah. You're crazy,'" Lisa recalled Rison's brother saying as they evacuated the house. Rison's friends then immediately went about smashing Lisa's car windows with pipes. She replied in kind by smashing the windows of his Mercedes-Benz and his truck.[6] Yet, even with the enormousness of her talent as a member of TLC and the fraught dynamic of her relationship with Rison, Lisa is still best remembered as an arsonist.

Two decades later, I wondered if the finale of Taylor Swift's music video for the 2014 hit "Blank Space," in which she sets her lover's mansion ablaze in a jealous rage, was a nod to Lopes. "Got a long list of ex-lovers / They'll tell you

I'm insane," she lilts in what would become the second-most-viewed video of all time on YouTube. The song and video are satirical takes on the media's treatment of Taylor as the model of the embittered, crazy ex-girlfriend and is largely responsible for 2014's being declared "The Year of the Crazy Ex-Girlfriend" by *Pitchfork*.[7] But it was a slow climb to that reclamation.

"Taylor Swift is a nutcase," Harvey Levin said of Swift's alleged propensity to buy property near her lovers in *Vanity Fair* in 2013.[8] "Her career depends on her getting laid and having her heart broken. That's what 99% of her songs are about. If we don't know who she's sleeping with, what else is there to really know about her? It's practically her job to always be in love with someone," wrote Ryan O'Connell on Thought Catalog in 2012.[9] Such statements litter the media coverage of Swift in her first few years as a pop singer, prompting first the question "Who the fuck are those dudes?" followed quickly by "What the fuck else do people write songs about if not who they're banging and having break their hearts?" Men certainly write on similar themes without being identified as insane.

Musician John Mayer owes much of his career to singing about heartbreak and famously wrote "Your Body Is a Wonderland" about onetime lover Jennifer Love Hewitt long before Taylor Swift was a household name. But Mayer told *Rolling Stone* in 2012 that he was "humiliated" by the song "Dear John" that Taylor wrote about him, which includes such damning lyrics as "Don't you think nineteen's too young to be played by your dark twisted games?" in reference to her age when they dated. "I will say as a songwriter that I think it's kind of cheap songwriting," he told the magazine two years after "Dear John" was released.[10] He would turn around and release the least thinly veiled response track, "Paper Doll," the following year. To date, however, he has not addressed whether or not nineteen is indeed too young to be played by his twisted games. Mayer is not the only ex who has let Taylor's success as a professional ex-girlfriend get under his skin. After nearly three years apart, even Taylor's fairly private ex Harry Styles of One Direction penned the lyrics, "If you're looking for someone to write your breakup songs about, then baby I'm perfect," on the 2015 single "Perfect."

The ascent of Taylor Swift and the reclamation of the "crazy ex-girlfriend" moniker as a term of power are indeed triumphs for women who have been unfairly labeled insane for even the slightest act of retribution. But she is not the quintessential crazy ex-girlfriend. Her particular madness is something most of us can relate to. We, too, have fantasized about the public humiliation of our exes and building reputations and fortunes out of the slights they have visited upon us. These types of "crazy" all seem so pedestrian when compared to the more substantial forms of retribution visited upon deserving husbands and lovers. It is a madness characterized not by brazen outbursts but by calculated silence. Their cunning and ability to play the long game to get what they want goes undetected. Their patience is formidable and their fortunes end up far more vast and real than the momentary pleasure of their ex's humiliation. But first, a close runner-up in the insane ex hall of fame: the espionage ex.

"I'll put you in a fucking rose garden, you cunt! You understand that? Because I'm capable of it. You understand that?" are among the more terrifying words that Mel Gibson had for his ex-wife Oksana Grigorieva in a 2010 phone call she recorded. During the call, he more or less admits to hitting her while she held their baby. Grigorieva recorded several conversations with Gibson, each one riddled with racial slurs and sexually violent degradations he fantasized about visiting upon her during the prolonged ending of their relationship. Gibson accused Grigorieva of editing the tapes and he pleaded for the public to understand the context of his anger, as though threatening murder and vocalizing gang rape fantasies is part and parcel of a typical breakup.[11] Many commentators agreed with Gibson and derided Grigorieva as an opportunist and a sexual manipulator. She was branded as the deeply loathed type of crazy ex-girlfriend concocted in the minds of men who believe that the mere fact of being a sexually desirable woman is a hostile act against men.

"Who anticipates being recorded? Who anticipates that? Who could anticipate such a personal betrayal?" Gibson would ask the following year in an interview with *Deadline Hollywood*.[12] The answer, of course, is a woman who knows that her word and even her wounds might be insufficient evidence at trial. A more reflective question might consider who anticipates having their safety threatened by someone they love. But Mel Gibson apparently had little time for logic or empathy. He would go on to plead no contest to a battery charge against Grigorieva, who was awarded a $750,000 settlement and a house to live in until their daughter turned eighteen. It was a paltry settlement compared to the size of Gibson's fortunes and an anticlimactic ending to the chaos of the preceding years. Throughout this turmoil, Mel Gibson's first wife lingered quietly off the radar.

Robyn Moore has a face that is familiar but difficult to place on its own. Few people would recognize her in a photograph if she was not standing next to Mel, the man to whom she was married for thirty-one years and with whom she had seven children. Mel Gibson enjoyed decades as a Hollywood favorite, accruing a massive fortune and a firmly rooted position on the A-list. That image began to fall apart after he was recorded spewing misogyny and anti-Semitism during a DUI arrest in 2006.[13] During the rant, he famously blamed all of the world's troubles on Jews and called a female officer "Sugar Tits." He then appealed to his own power when he sneered, "I own Malibu...I am going to fuck you." When news surfaced that he'd had two previous encounters with law enforcement that were dismissed by local police, it became clear that this was not a sad one-off but the case of a man accustomed to getting what he wanted and raising hell if it was not given to him.[14] He and Moore quietly separated after the incident, the emphasis on *quiet* belonging to Robyn entirely, as Mel made the media rounds apologizing and excusing his behavior.

Though many were shocked by the recording, Mel's bigotry and the cheap shots and bullying in which it manifested were not well-kept secrets so much as they were tolerated truths. In 1991, he made homophobic comments that were printed in the Spanish newspaper *El País*, pointing at his own ass and saying, "This is only for taking a shit."[15] Four years later, after considerable time for reflection, he told *Playboy* that he would apologize for this and other comments, "when hell freezes over."[16] When Frank Rich at the *New York Times* gave *The Passion of the Christ* a negative review, Mel said he wanted to have Rich's intestines on a stick and to kill the man's dog.[17] Yet Moore stood by her man throughout this time, smiling on red carpets and presumably running an impeccable household. After three years of separation, Robyn filed for divorce when news of Grigorieva's pregnancy became public in 2009.

From the outside, it appears to have all been a quiet, dignified proceeding. Moore has been a paragon of silence except in one instance where she signed a sworn statement, declaring that Gibson had never abused her or their children during their marriage, that was presented in proceedings for Grigorieva's case against Gibson.[18] During their own divorce, Gibson and Moore made joint statements about maintaining their family's privacy and integrity in a difficult time, but the final judgment was certainly a blow to Mel Gibson's finances. Robyn walked away with $425 million, half of her ex-husband's fortunes, making it the largest divorce settlement in Hollywood history. Robyn is also entitled to half the film residuals Mel Gibson earns for the rest of his life on films made during their marriage.[19] Once the divorce settlement was finalized, mentions of Robyn vanished almost entirely from news media.

What indignities the demure and attractive wife endured during their decades of marriage will likely remain unknown. Her silence makes it tempting to project ideas onto her as a calculating plotter, lying in wait for the right moment to walk off into the sunset with almost a half billion dollars, never to be heard from again. I consider the unbridled anger of a man like Mel Gibson as he took it out on individual reporters and police and entire racial and religious groups. I have doubts that such frothing rage can be so easily extinguished when crossing over the threshold of his home, rendering it a tranquil sanctuary.

When I witnessed Gibson's humiliating encounters with law enforcement and his ex-wife when I was younger, I would think of the embarrassment of his seven children, several of whom are close in age to me. Today, I think of his silent, smiling wife Robyn. I don't assume to know the heart of Robyn Moore, but I can imagine that it took an almost pathological commitment to forgiveness and patience to last as long as she did. She stood by for such events until at last they were too much. I wonder, too, what the weight of keeping Mel Gibson's secrets costs her. Robyn's particular brand of retribution goes mostly undetected by the crude radars presently policing women's behaviors because it is so tremendously skilled. Were it detected, she might be among the most vilified of all the crazy exes because of the nature of what she walked away with.

The common thread that weaves throughout these stories spanning time and socioeconomic stations and even international borders is not that these women's actions were crazy, even loosely defined. Their crimes were in committing actions and seizing assets that are considered the exclusive entitlements of men. These are the objects that are believed to transfer status and prosperity to men. When women take them into their own hands out of either destructive impulses or wills to power, they must be dismissed as insane. They violated the sacred and highly gendered order of things and must be dismissed as aberrations. Diana smashing china to bits with a hammer looks irrational only when a woman's body performs the destructive deed. When men destroy property in a fit, it is considered an acceptable expression of male rage. Some even find it arousing. Lorena Bobbitt took perhaps the most literal entitlement from a man: his own penis, which doubled as a weapon in their relationship. She seized control of it and deflated its power by removing it from the source of its power. And though Aaliyah never famously feuded with R. Kelly, I still like to think that it was something of a slap in the face that she did not let his manipulation and control define her and went on to an all-too-brief but still brilliant career.

Lopes's burning a house down was not just a subversion of the fact that most arsonists are men but was the destruction of property, that precious commodity that for so long was owned exclusively by men. She burned his birthright to the ground. Taylor Swift has no literally destructive impulses, but her active destabilization of the music industry expectation that women are to be pining and lovesick by being sneering and hell-bent on revenge is another kind of destruction. It certainly wounded the egos of men like John Mayer, who went crying to tabloids over Taylor's betrayal; this from a man who famously called Jessica Simpson "sexual napalm" and wrote a song about Jennifer Love Hewitt's anatomy. That Taylor has amassed far more wealth in the process is still another way she has gone insane, turning men into muses that profit her rather than the other way around. And then there are the strong, silent wives like Robyn whose hearts are the safe havens for the secrets of men who have likely done far more unspeakable wrongs than we could ever know. They sacrifice much by not exposing the terrors of these men, but they are handsomely rewarded with the massive fortunes that men have controlled and used to nurture their own power for centuries.

I think of these women often when a man calls a woman a crazy ex-girlfriend as an insult, unaware that identifying a woman this way elevates her to a rogue hero of her gender rather than a disgrace to it. This growing cohort of crazy exes have sacrificed much to get where they are and to be given what they are owed. Many of my personal heroes from this particular canon are no longer alive. May they rest in power. But I am hopeful, too, that as more baby girls come up in the world, they will accept the burden of power we deserve and nurture it well so that it becomes undeniably their own. And then when no one is expecting them to, they will crack it open and take everything they were owed from it. I want these baby girls to live in a world where they know that once "bitch" and "crazy" have been taken back into our custody for good, it is time to come for the world.

Emparadised

On Joan Didion and Personal Mythology as Survival

E MPARADISED" IS A WORD USED to describe how the deserts of Southern California were transformed into the lush tree-lined cities we know today by enterprising gardeners and city planners. I read it once on a gardening website I don't know how I got to because I have never gardened, but I liked the word and kept it with me to describe the place I come from. Memories of my adolescence in San Diego were of people with good looks and bad politics, impossibly bronzed residents dotting a landscape of adobe tract houses, endless highways, and strip malls designed by people whose experience of Mexican architecture is limited to the "It's a Small World" attraction at Disneyland. I used the word to describe Southern California when I was vowing never to return.

The first time I reconsidered this vow I was lying on the beach at Silver Sands State Park in Connecticut. I had checked out a stack of books by mystical poets and a selection of women writers whose only shared characteristics were tasteful aloofness and thinness that lingers at the border between elegance and illness. Joan Didion, the reigning queen of this literary class, naturally featured heavily in the stack. It was the summer between my first and second years as a graduate student at Yale Divinity School where I was pursuing a Master of Arts in Religion, but it was by accident that I selected Didion's novel *Play It as It Lays*, a book whose primary tensions center on evil and nothingness. The decision to apply to and enroll in divinity school was one of many haphazard attempts to seek the substance of my own suffering in books, though exploring questions of evil was a secondary benefit to my expensive exercise in self-discovery. My roommate there had once told me that hell, that infernal holding cell for evil, is simply the absence of God. It is nothing. *Play It as It Lays* more or less corroborated this explanation. It satisfied me.

This was a few years shy of that period of Joan Didion mania, followed soon by fatigue, a time between 2013 and 2015 when several publications of note were overrun with material about the author that culminated in a review of her biography in the *Atlantic*, which momentarily entertained the grim idea that "for all her brilliance, she might be deemed too haughty to tolerate, the ultimate white girl."[1] We were suddenly bombarded with stories on the literary and societal significance of Joan, two biographies of her were released, a Kickstarter campaign for a documentary about her was funded in record time, and the octogenarian Joan herself starred in a campaign for the elite fashion line Céline. Haley Mlotek at the *Hairpin* described the campaign as the convergence of two "mental shortcuts": Joan as the patron saint of well-read white women in their twenties and Céline as a signifier for a discerning aesthetic eye for minimalist design, if not a bank account for purchasing said designs. Mlotek wrote, "I didn't feel trolled because Céline was mocking me, or us, but because I had been so thoroughly and effectively target marketed, an experience that is like being a deer in branded headlights. *We've been seen!* I panicked. *They know too much!*"[2]

But that day on the beach in 2011 was before all that, or at least before I knew it. Back then, adoring Joan Didion was a private devotion that I could indulge without the attendant self-consciousness that comes with being too caught up in a cultural moment to really enjoy it. And so I recklessly imbued her fiction with images of Joan herself. I imagined the protagonist Maria Wyeth as physically identical to her, inserting her into the scenes as an avatar inspired by the many photos of Joan where she is either leaning onto or out of a car. Though the photos rarely indicate the actual climate, they have hints of the desert complemented by her disinterested expression that never quite becomes a scowl. She smokes cigarettes indoors in several, too, a tragically lost art I've dared to engage in only while drunk or alone. Her words are known to conjure strong emotions in her readers, but Joan herself remains inscrutable. Fusing the attractive fiction of Joan established in my mind with the interior life of Maria Wyeth as set out on the page made a superheroine to imitate so that I might replace the effusive, clumsily emotive woman I was.

In the story, California is a state that comprises not gated communities and spray tans but extramarital affairs between film producers and impressively ambivalent women. It is a state connected by battered highways guarded by wizened amphibians, and the sordid mysteries of a destination where everyone has come to escape from someplace else. I envied Maria her sparse but carefully chosen words; I coveted the remarks people made about her weighing too little and being standoffish to the point of pathology. Maria appeared to feel so little and I felt so very much. At ten o'clock each day, she would set out for long drives, with the highway a destination unto itself.

The novel starts with Maria's narration, "What makes Iago evil? some people ask. I never ask." It is unclear if she is afraid to ask, if she already knows the answer, or if she doesn't care. If it were not for this uncertainty about evil and the nervous breakdown that an abortion prompts in the story, one might assume Maria to be a sociopath. But even in the tumult of an unplanned pregnancy when she casually reports to her husband that she doesn't know whose baby she's carrying, she remains ice even in the desert. The story is littered with men attempting to police her emotions while forgiving their own undeveloped ones. She finds them tiresome. I liked this trait of hers then and I like it now, in no small part because I am so hopelessly drawn to such men. Her web of extramarital

---

affairs with moneyed men and high stakes were not situations into which I could easily insert the characters in my own life, but it didn't stop me from trying. From a very young age, I always wanted to find myself among the thinnest and most unceremoniously sad girls.

I read especially memorable passages aloud to my boyfriend Michael over the course of three days at the beach when I read the book. It was in the hope that his palpable lack of interest in me that summer would dissolve in the face of the precious but melancholy habit of wide-eyed girls reading sad stories out loud. When it did not work, I attempted to adopt the cool, unfeeling demeanor of my protagonist, who had affairs with the same thoughtlessness with which she might make toast, were she ever inclined to eat any. But try as I might, I could not beat Michael at ambivalence that summer. And so I retreated deeper into the desert landscape from whence I came to find shelter from his neglect.

I finished the book on July 4, 2011. I remember it because the beach was evacuated to look for a missing man and child. We went home when the evacuation went into its second hour. That night we fought on the way to the fireworks atop East Rock Park in New Haven and I watched the show in tears, standing next to him but not daring to touch him in a gesture of reconciliation. As Michael drove us down through winding roads out of the darkened woods of the park, a voice on the radio announced that earlier in the day, a man had tried to walk across the sandbar that stretched from the beach at Silver Sands to Charles Island but was swept away by a wave and drowned. The nine-year-old boy who was with him was rescued, thanks to the combined efforts of a lifeguard and a jet skier. The man who died was named Rocco. He was thirty-four years old.

I would learn at the end of the summer, just two days before signing a new lease with Michael, that he had spent the summer relapsed on a variety of opiates. We had met the year before when he was two weeks out of rehab, which was two more weeks of sobriety than I had. From the vantage point of a single day clean, his two weeks might as well have been a lifetime. It took another year and a half for things to end between us but not because of anything nearly so sexy as opiate dependence. It was the far more ordinary crisis of an apartment we were planning to rent falling through at the last minute due to credit issues Michael accrued while on heroin before he met me. All of our issues subsequently collapsed into the vacant space to which we now could not relocate. I moved out on my own and lost weight as an act of aggression. I still wonder if he ever realized that in addition to all of the heavy emotional lifting I did in that time and in all of our time together, I permanently dedicated thirty pounds of myself to him. Thanks to the breakup, I saw my lifelong goal of achieving worry-inducing thinness in a matter of months. Maria and I were getting closer.

In the summer of 2013, Michael asked if he could send me a birthday present. It was six months since we had broken up, and he'd asked as a gesture of his respect for my boundaries as we considered giving it another shot. I arrived home from my twenty-eighth birthday party to find a mailbox full of package notices for gifts from my family that I would have to go to the post office to fetch the following day and one small package from Michael. I was tired from a three-mile walk home following dinner with a small group of friends from whom I'd grown apart while I was away at Yale and never fully reconnected with upon my return to Brooklyn. The group grew noticeably smaller each year, as birthday parties become the private stuff one mourns with their inner circle rather than the public celebrations of our very existence they are in younger years.

I was happy to have at least Michael's gift to open on my birthday and so I tore into the manila envelope with the shameless urgency of a child. It was a paperback copy of *Play It as It Lays* and a note recalling my fondness for Joan Didion and his near certainty that I hadn't read this one, but that it sounded like something I might like. The cover featured a photograph of a thin woman sprawled out in a sleeveless white dress. The top half of her face is out of the frame, and her body is loose in a way that indicates the kind of lethargy induced by hard drugs rather than the rest of sleep. The gift was a sweet but unknowingly cruel gesture, a postcard from the isolated hell of that sticky and stinking summer cohabitating with a ghost I could not rouse back to life by pitifully reading book passages aloud. The realization that my vivid memories of reading this very book to him were not shared by him made me resolute in the decision not to rekindle the relationship. Anger that had mostly subsided reignited in the knowledge that even on those rare occasions that he would lie down by my side that summer, I had still actually been alone. It was too eerie a coincidence that the book title was a gambling reference while considering giving a chance to a man whose track record inspired so little confidence.

The next day I put the book on the top shelf of my bookcase, too high to see the title when I passed the shelf and remember all over again. Then I went to pick up the packages my family sent. Among them was a white tulle party dress from my sister. I did not realize it at the time, but it bore a remarkable similarity to the dress on the cover of *Play It as It Lays*. I was not yet looking for omens. Though I knew before I left that I would be overdressed, I wore it to a barbecue that my friend Tommy was having for his twenty-ninth birthday at his family home in Brooklyn. Had I noted the similarity earlier, I might have noticed more coincidences in the events and catastrophes to come.

At the party I sat stiffly on a patio chair and listened quietly while the men present spoke about the state of their industries and cooked with fire. I spoke when spoken to, except when I was politely offering to carry food items between the kitchen and the backyard, then back again as needed. My offer was always declined, and so I was subjected to pointed questions by Tommy's well-meaning but prodding father, whom I knew from church. "Do you miss your family?" he asked when I reported that they were still in San Diego and that I visited rarely. "No," I told him, failing to give even a moment's pause to reflect on how heartless this truth would sound.

When the hosts disappeared inside and a silence briefly hovered over the patio, a young man with unkempt blond hair and smoke in his voice said, "What are you doing over there? You're too pretty to be sitting by yourself like that. Come here." It was a moment that confirms the worst fears of a certain type of bitter and ordinary male: that their bad pickup lines are usually bad because the man saying them is ordinary. On the lips and in the throats of handsome men, they are a charm attack. I turned my eyes without turning my head and smiled with only half my mouth, a literary move from California in 1970 if one ever existed. The young man's name was not James, but I will call him that here, just as I call everyone here by a different name. It was the first time of many that I would come to him when he called me.

Within the hour, James and I were snorting crushed Valium and Percocet in the basement of Tommy's family home. He introduced the existence of his girlfriend by telling me that his instinct as I leaned over to snort lines was to hold back my hair but that his girlfriend wouldn't like that. I said, "It's just hair," feigning the nonchalance I was perfecting more quickly now that I had been single for some time. I didn't mean a word of the three words. We had unprotected sex pressed up against the bathroom counter as the song "Thrift Shop" by Macklemore throbbed on the porch above us.

By nightfall, we were with Tommy and two of their friends on the road to a cabin in the Hudson Valley, where the party would continue through the weekend. It was three days of sex on icy riverbanks, in the back of his truck, and, in an especially poor judgment call, in the parking lot of a gun supply store. The shelter of the deep woods made us candid. And just as Maria's parents were reduced to a reckless gambling father and a mother crippled by neurosis, we, too, spoke of one-dimensional fathers whom we feared we disappointed and of mothers made almost entirely of love and poorly executed good intentions.

He was a native New Yorker and I had been an enthusiastic import when I was eighteen, so we recounted the many merits of the city while deriding Los Angeles, where his job in the entertainment industry often sent him. He spoke of the terrible artifice of Los Angeles and I echoed the sentiments with a litany of San Diego's moral and urban-planning failures. It was a perfect set of circumstances in which to start an affair and a lousy one in which to fall in love.

"You can be my girlfriend that knows about my girlfriend," James suggested on the ride home on Monday. He smiled with his whole face from the driver's seat, grasping at my left hand with his right. He demanded that Tommy, our affair's new coconspirator, plug his ears while he began negotiations for how we might continue our illicit behavior upon our return to the city. I felt like I was ten years old again, when my first boyfriend, Scott, made his friend Kurt go into the closet so that my dignity would remain intact for our first kiss. James sulked convincingly at my refusal of the offer. "It just sounds very French to me," I replied coyly, a line that made him laugh. To this day, I am still not sure if I stole that line from a book.

Like Maria Wyeth, I was in a habit of sleeping with attached men. But this was the first time I had done so knowingly on the first try and the first time that I had wanted to continue despite the fact. But when we arrived at my apartment and unloaded my bags from the truck bed where we had been fucking just a few hours before, I averted eye contact and slowly said my phone number so he could enter it into his phone without Tommy being able to tell from the passenger seat. "I'm going to see you," he said, staring directly at my eyes though I kept them averted. "You have my number," I replied, in the hopes that a value-neutral response would drive him crazy about me.

His barrage of attention and affection began two days later. He said that he missed me and wanted to see me at the end of the week. He had a way with words and a swagger I had seen only in movies. I remained careful not to let delight come across my face when I was so convincingly feeling so very little. At one point, Joan describes a masseur and Maria's dear friend BZ as "gleaming, unlined, as if they had an arrangement with mortality." It is a physical description but one apt for how I saw James: a spot of eternity in an otherwise rotting world.

James often remarked on the oddness of how even military personnel and law enforcement were drawn to him. "I don't get it; they just like me for some reason," he would say, especially during the conversations we'd have when he asked to meet my career Navy veteran father. In a mix of envy and awe I would reply, "That's because everybody likes you." He would shrug off such claims, unaware of his charisma's attendant privileges and I unwilling to expand on their power.

We began to meet often at his parents' Battery Park City apartment overlooking the Hudson River. It was infrequently occupied since his parents had retired to what he referred to as "Long Island" but I would later learn was East Hampton. It was one of many attempts to obscure the extent of the wealth in which he was raised, but the address and even the sheets on the bed that always smelled fresh in their immaculate whiteness betrayed a story of money. The apartment was not characterized by its value so much as its seeming ability to stop time. In one fantasy in the novel, Maria injects sodium pentothal, or "truth serum," into her arm. When it fails she imagines driving into the "hard white empty core of the world." Being with James felt like some euphoric combination of both; only the white empty core was not so desolate and desperate when our modern prescription variations of sodium pentothal were able to populate it with what I believed to be some sad but true thing at the center of us.

At a birthday party toward the end of the summer I told a friend about his more worrying habits. In an attempt to disguise my growing affection, I said, "Don't worry, he's just a rich kid posturing as a graduate of the School of the Hard Knocks." Without missing a beat, she replied, "That's always the one that dies first in the movies." There were warning signs all over, first in their eyes and then in the few brave enough to summon the word "unhealthy" to their lips.

We returned to the Hudson Valley near the end of the summer for an informal folk music gathering that Tommy's family throws every year. James had broken up with his girlfriend by then, but another ex of his, Virginia, would be making an appearance with two friends he was not aware of until a few hours before her arrival. He berated Tommy for allowing Virginia to come, venomous and snide in a way I had not yet witnessed in him. I sat silently in the front of the truck as he banged on the steering wheel and rattled off irrelevant but embarrassing personal details about the trio of young women and the traitorous friends who had granted them passage. I had heard of Virginia before only in passing, a "crazy ex" with whom things had not ended well. I was accustomed to this lazy shorthand for men who dislike the emotions of women, but his outrage signified that she still meant something to him. Men do not indulge in such outbursts over women about whom they are ambivalent.

I soothed myself with literary snapshots of men's violent outbursts representing some internal passion, disfigured care but care nonetheless. Carter and Maria might fight this way, I thought. "After that he would leave for a while, breaking things as he went, slamming doors to kick them open, picking up decanters to hurl at mirrors, detouring by way of chairs to smash them against the floor. Always when he came back he would sleep in their room, shutting the door against her. Rigid with self-pity she would lie in another room, wishing for the will to leave," Joan writes of the fights between Maria and her husband. We were in the open woods and sharing the back of a truck, so I had the refuge of rigidity but not of another room, which felt like enough to last a weekend.

My discomfort at the speed and force of his unexpected wrath prompted me to drink for the first time in three years. I became drunk quickly, from both lack of practice and from the anxieties that had prompted me to imbibe in the first place. Virginia and her friends introduced themselves to me kindly, while James avoided the section of the woods where they had set up camp. In the absence of my typical inhibitions, I enthusiastically befriended them and found them warmer. Their designer clothing and casual talk of international travel suggested wealth similar to James's, but they did not posture against it as he did.

The only photograph of James and me together would be taken during that hazy episode. In the photo, I am staring into the camera, desperately drunk, with my mouth half open and a come-hither stare. James's back is turned to the camera behind me, adding wood to a massive bonfire. I have attempted to project meaning into this scene, something about my negligence that he was building an attractive and dangerous fire within my sights. It never quite sticks as well as the simple fact that I wanted to stand by the fire and he wanted to build it.

The two of us drove home together at the end of the weekend and stopped for dinner around dusk. After a long silence, he took my hand in his and said, "I want us to go to Cozumel. I want to take you to Cozumel." It was a place I knew well from photos taken by my friends who remained in

San Diego into adulthood, but I had never been myself. I also knew it to be a desirable destination because BZ's mother in the story hates it, and what glimpses of her the reader gets are terrifically unflattering. I replied, "So let's go," but knew very well that James would never take me to Cozumel.

He would break things off with me two weeks later to attempt to repair the relationship that we had poisoned with our basement antics and the events that followed. He even asked for advice on getting her back a day after professing once again how much he missed me. I treated the pain of being unchosen with Klonopin and a solo viewing of a One Direction documentary at the Kent Theater on Coney Island Avenue. It was my budget version of driving off into the great white nothing of the desert; and in lieu of a handsome actor to fuck some of the pain away, I settled for the on-screen company of cheerful, rambunctious boys.

When James reemerged in November, it was with appeals to the woods. He texted that he missed "getting high and wilding." He communicated the way a teenager might, tearing at the fabric of the very adult tragedy I felt I was living. I said that if he was serious about seeing me, he would have to come over that very night to prove it. It was the resolute ultimatum of a grown woman masking a childish enthusiasm at the potential reunion. He arrived within the hour. Two weeks later, he claimed to have ended things completely with his girlfriend. We picked up right where we left off.

I made him promise that if he ever chose someone over me again, he would not tell me. He should just break things

ALL THE LIVES I WANT

off and go away, make another excuse if necessary. I told him that girlfriends don't just sprout from the ground and that the devastation of being left for someone else would be more to bear than the knowledge that he'd continue to sleep with other people. I also asked to never be complicit in his infidelity again. I felt that I had outgrown other-womanhood and did not want to play the role. Frankly, I felt too much and let it show.

I hesitated to share my writing with James, considering it an earnest collection that was at odds with my nonchalant self-presentation and intentional air of mystery. But in the early morning of the Fourth of July, I laid my head in his lap and pulled up a segment that I had written and read for a CBC radio show. The story was about my struggle with suicidal ideation and a saccharine reflection on our belovedness by strangers. I was quick to share the story with the whole of Canada, but my fingers trembled as I pressed Play for the man I loved despite myself. It was after an all-night run through several bags of cocaine and the director's cut of *Apocalypse Now*. The all-nighter was full of our typical laughter and near-perfect sex, but our serotonin-starved brains after so much cocaine and so little sleep left us vulnerable as the segment played.

"That was really beautiful," he said after seven excruciating minutes spent listening to my own voice. He kissed my forehead and said he was glad I was alive. "Why don't you ever write about me? About us?" he asked. I said that I wrote about people only with their permission and asked why he wanted me to anyway. "I don't know. To prove that we mattered. To prove that we existed," James replied. I recalled a moment of frustration between Maria and her friend BZ over her seeming ambivalence. "Tell me what matters," BZ had demanded of her. "Nothing." Maria's reply was decidedly sharper than mine, but I said, "James, we don't exist." In my perfect version of women having their emotions entirely obscured under bored gazes, neither of us would have bothered to respond at all.

That evening, we went to a barbecue on his sister's roof in Crown Heights. Having primarily witnessed his charm in groups of strangers, I was startled by the blinding love between James and his family and friends. It was his typical charm on steroids, amplified by the familiarity of the crowd and by the celebratory nature of the holiday. Through nervous laughter and averted eye contact, I fumbled through introductions and withheld tears as he held me close during the fireworks. I thought briefly about how there were worse ways to spend the Fourth of July. At the bottom of the Long Island Sound between the beach at Silver Sands and Charles Island, for example. The next morning, I broke things off and gave him my e-mail address, "in case you need to let me know about any STIs," I said, in yet another attempt to appear as empty as I longed to be.

My no-contact resolution did not last long. I sent him photos of myself in a sequined bikini, purple on top and green on the bottom to resemble a mermaid. There was a failed attempt to coordinate schedules so that we'd be in New Orleans at the same time. I refused to meet him and held on to hope that some new man who was also charm incarnate would appear so that I might never see James again. "I want to *see* you," he would whine convincingly, appealing to a certain fondness I had for occasional turns of boyishness. He requested more photos, and I refused as a sort of pregaming for disciplinary role-play. One night would have been a typical exchange of plans to get together littered with explicit photos, but then James told me that he'd be moving to Los Angeles to be with someone else. "There was a silence. Something real was happening: this was, as it were, her life. If she could keep that in mind she would be able to play it through, do the right thing, whatever that meant," Joan writes.

I put up a worthy fight against his insistence on seeing me one last time before he left. He tried to coax me into forgiveness for what I knew would be his final abandonment. He said, "I love you," for the first time and refused my request that he take it back. We exchanged the kind of cruelty reserved for those we know how to cut the deepest. He walked out the door and bid me farewell in a text message rather than with the smoke in his voice.

"Fuck it, I said to them all, a radical surgeon of my own life," Maria declares at one point. "Radical surgeon of my own life" was a line I had remembered and conjured often, long before retrofitting this story about the desert to a city affair. But what happened next was not so much a delicate surgery on myself but rather a crude execution of any lingering love left between us. I found his new girlfriend online and told her everything. He retaliated with a swift and relentless viciousness that would be more an exercise in trauma pornography than in prose to deliver here. His desire to hear my bones crushed under a moving train and a gentle declaration that I'd be pretty with a bullet in my head made appearances alongside actual threats. He asked over and over why I did it.

"I am what I am. To look for 'reasons' is beside the point," Maria says, protesting the very idea of pursuing explanations. I admit that I fumbled over and wept into explanations for my reasons when he called to spew venom like the very snakes that litter the story to which I now return so often when I replay this episode. "I had to burn every fiber of every bridge that led to you," I choked out through tears, proud to have introduced metaphor even in a time of great distress. The truth was more complicated, more hostile. After all, I was like Maria, and "[she] did not particularly believe in rewards, only in punishments, swift and personal."

When his new girlfriend stood fast in her refusal to speak to him, he claimed he had taken thirty Klonopin and his imminent death would be my fault because I took his love away. When he stopped responding to my texts, I begged her to talk to him again so he'd go to a hospital, which she did. In hindsight, faking an overdose was a brilliant Trojan horse to ride back into her life on. It was then that he was able to rewrite our history as just one of many affairs he regretted with the sad, sundry bulimics of New York. He left for Los Angeles the next day.

There were moments to which I returned repeatedly in the aftermath, trying to match his calculated deceit to prior conversations that he used to gather intel. His professed desire to have only daughters mirrored my own, but I was unsure if it had been gleaned from a direct statement of preference or from my evident distrust of men. He began to tell me, "I just want you to feel safe with me," several weeks after I revealed past violence experienced at the hands of men. He pulled me into the nook of his arm and whispered, "I want to keep you here forever where it's safe." I wondered what it felt like to possess such emotional capital and not use it. I wondered if the burden of latent antipathy felt similar to latent passion.

There are times, too, when I am drawn back into the text of *Play It as It Lays* and find new ways of having inhabited the story without my own knowledge. "By the end of the week she was thinking constantly about where her body stopped and the air began, about the exact point in space and time that was the difference between *Maria* and *other*," Joan writes of Maria's extended trip to Las Vegas, a feeling of disorientation that characterized the weeks that followed. On one of her routine drives into the desert, Joan writes, "As if in a trance Maria watched the woman, for it seemed to her then that she was watching the dead still center of the world, the quintessential intersection of nothing." It was this feeling that I clung to in the aftermath, having felt what I thought was love coursing through the marrow in my bones only to discover poison in the end.

But the artifacts and gestures of our time together were hollow things shaped like love, their true emotional bankruptcy revealed by touch rather than by sight. They were hyperrealistic portraits and bowls of plastic fruit rather than blurry landscapes that appeared whole from afar. Part of the purpose of such objects is illusion itself; they are designed not only to appear beautiful but to appear *real*.

The archive that remains of me and James is littered with artifacts well suited to melancholy fiction. Condom wrappers behind a heating unit and cocaine residue on a hardcover children's book. The address in Battery Park City stuck stubbornly in the memory of my takeout delivery account. An armchair that he moved into my apartment for me and then sat in for a lap dance. A matching pink-and-yellow bra and G-string, a sartorial abomination to me, but sex appeal to him. There is a collection of screenshots of text messages in which I halfheartedly sever ties, followed by his uncharacteristically quick replies with empty promises to do better. I am not the first person guilty of saying, "I'm leaving now," when I really mean, "Don't you want me to stay?"

I made it all the way to the process of transcribing his threats on an official form for requesting an order of protection at the courthouse in downtown Brooklyn before realizing that because he fled so quickly to Los Angeles, there would be no way of delivering it without his address. I am glad I was spared the bureaucratic nightmare of pursuing it to its end. I am told that is its own kind of trauma. I am happy to have conjured the strength to deny him an opportunity to bear witness to my suffering again. I have no way of knowing if Los Angeles quieted his restless and reckless tendencies. I have no way of knowing if he was lying when we lay in his truck and spoke such ill of the Golden State. I do hope that he is sufficiently distracted by paradise.

I told a friend from Yale Divinity School about the episode early in the winter that followed as we made the case to ourselves that New York was the best city to live in on earth and that Southern California was a destination for moral failures. She recommended a text by Thomas Merton, a mystic I had read on days when no one died on the beach and therefore had allowed to let slip away from my memory more easily. He wrote:

> Yet look at the deserts today. What are they? The birthplace of a new and terrible creation, the testing ground of the power by which man seeks to un-create what God has blessed. Today, in the century of man's greatest technological achievement, the wilderness at last comes into its own...He can build there his fantastic, protected cities of withdrawal and experimentation and vice...They are brilliant and sordid smiles of the devil upon the face of the wilderness, cities of secrecy where each man spies on his brother, cities through whose veins money runs like artificial blood, and from whose womb will come the last and greatest instrument of destruction.

I stop short of agreeing with this account entirely, because to suggest that James is the anti-Christ is to give him too much credit. When I had been afraid in the aftermath of his threats, my friend Phoebe, whose name is the only real one used in this story, told me with remarkable certainty, "That man is a loser who will never accomplish anything, including your murder." She was right. I am a small person inside and out, and he couldn't even destroy me, much less civilization. But I can return to that brilliant sordid smile resting on a face that did not betray the wasteland beneath it and still be unnerved by its cruel forgery.

In Los Angeles, the city marches on as a permanent paradise, a facade that requires it to desperately pump water in from other regions to nurture the foreign flora that make it so appealing an imitation of life. It is a city that was literally built to construct lies upon, the old photographs of movie sets of brilliant cities set against the background of a desert betraying the unreality of its current beauty. It is then that I am grateful for the brutal and increasingly endless New York winters that crack the skin to the point of bleeding, proving the existence of a beating heart below.

Like Maria on her drives into the desert, I picked up a habit of running to the Atlantic at 4 a.m. along Ocean Parkway in Brooklyn. The destination is Coney Island but only because it happens to be at the edge of the city; it is there in the morning lights that I am often struck again by a parallel to the story in my own life. It is there that I have resisted my resistance to feeling too heavily reliant on writers like Joan and the women they breathe something like life into to give a narrative arc to my life, to make it more than nothing. To still play. Of *Play It as It Lays*, she said specifically that it is "a white book to which the reader would have to bring his or her own bad dreams." And so it is where I put my collection of bad dreams, both the ones that I lived and the ones that came to me in my sleep. And so I think of that birthday week and the tulle dress and the man with smoke in his voice as the time I thought I was abandoning the cunning appeal of a sleek and serpentine desert, but was actually stumbling into it.

I return often to the woods and how sincere James had seemed when he proclaimed the superiority of the city of his birth. He said he would stay forever, as if he were not only the city's proud resident, but its heir apparent. But Joan also said, in her book *The White Album*, "A place belongs forever to whoever claims it hardest, remembers it most obsessively, wrenches it from itself, shapes it, renders it, loves it so radically that he remakes it in his own image." And I have loved New York more radically by staying, by giving it more credit than it deserves because it is more easily broken than the desert because it is has more life within it. It is at dawn, looking into the blackness of the Atlantic, feeling the harsh winds and witnessing the unforgiving tides that bring a chill to the city, that I feel this place belongs to me now. And it is then that I am certain I dwell on a safer shore.

Acknowledgments

I am forever grateful for the steadying confidence and saintly patience that my agent, Adriann Ranta, had in my work long before anyone else had either. To witness Libby Burton's ability to combine the editorial precision of a surgeon with an exuberant confidence in me rivaled only by my own mother's was an honor and a privilege. The team at Grand Central Publishing, including production editor Carolyn Kurek, copy editor Deborah Wiseman, along with Lisa Honerkamp, Shelby Howick, and Caitlin Mulrooney-Lyski, who have echoed Libby's enthusiasm and support with their work to make this book possible, has moved me profoundly. I can only hope to repay them in kind.

I want to thank my parents, Gail and Robert Massey, for eschewing the parental tradition of steering children away from creative professions and being the first true believers in my stories. My sister, Nova Massey, has been a source of love I can fold into and the only rock I am allowed to crash against as many times as I need. To the sisters I found later in life, Phoebe Anderson, Natasha Lennard, Alana Levinson, and Charlotte Shane: Your kind hearts and fierce minds are miracles the world hasn't earned but I'm glad it has in it anyway. Craig Reynolds, I am so grateful that we found each other as I was stranded in the middle of this process and that your love and confidence brought me safely to the other shore.

To Olivia Hall and Evan Derkacz, the first editors who ever took a chance on a writer with the disjointed interests and the out-of-place divinity school degree: Thank you for taking a chance and for remaining strange. To my editors at BuzzFeed, Doree Shafrir, Arianna Rebolini, and Isaac Fitzgerald: Thank you for molding my essays into shapes that resonated with audiences I never knew how to reach.

To the small army of friends and supporters I have in my life willing to read my drafts, humor my rambling pitch ideas, and reply thoughtfully to my text message scrolls of insecurity and frustration: You have meant the world to me and helped me make my place in the world. So thank you, Lola Pellegrino, Kate D'Adamo, Emily Genetta, Melissa Gira Grant, Morgan Jerkins, Rachel Syme, Rachel Vorona Cote, Arabelle Sicardi, Cheyenne Picardo, Taina Martinez, Mychal Denzel Smith, Maria Bowler, John McElwee, Paul Lucas, Safy-Hallan Farah, Heather Havrilesky, Molly Crabapple, Matt Stupp, Suzan Eraslan, Rebecca Traister, Ashley Ford, Ryan Jacobs, Fariha Roisin, Meghan Daigneau, Lauren Clyne, Meaghan O'Connell, and so many more whom I have forgotten and will realize the moment I reread this list in print.

And finally, to the women who star in this book: Thanks for being a more stunning, ferocious, and wild gang of imaginary friends than I could ever dream up myself.

Notes

Being Winona; Freeing Gwyneth

1   Amelie Gillette, "Gwyneth Paltrow Finds Noted Music-maker William Joel Just Delightful," A.V. Club, 11 June 2009, http://www.avclub.com/article/gwyneth-paltrow-finds-noted-music-maker-william-jo-29101.

2   Dodai Stewart, "Gwyneth Paltrow Wants to Hire You!", *Jezebel*, 2 June 2011, http://jezebel.com/5807846/gwyneth-paltrow-wants-to-hire-you.

3   *Tonight Show with Jay Leno* with Winona Ryder, Dailymotion, http://www.dailymotion.com/video/x134cik_tonight-show-with-jay-leno-with-winona-ryder_shortfilms.

4   Dylan Howard, "The Top Thirty Secrets and Scandals Gwyneth Paltrow Doesn't Want You to Know About," RadarOnline, 3 December 2015, http://radaronline.com/photos/gwyneth-paltrow-secrets-exposed-vanity-fair-takedown/photo/585157/.

Public Figures

1   Ashley Ross, "Britney Does It Again," *Shape*, June 2013, http://www.shape.com/blogs/fit-famous/britney-does-it-again-june-issue-shape.

2   Kyle Buchanan, "Crisis Averted: Jessica Simpson Defuses Rumor That Poppa Joe Fit Her for Training Bra," *Gawker*, 24 June 2008, http://gawker.com/5019297/crisis-averted-jessica-simpson-defuses-rumor-that-poppa-joe-fit-her-for-training-bra.

3   "How Britney Lost Her Baby Weight," *People*, 20 October 2006, http://celebritybabies.people.com/2006/10/20/how_britney_los/.

4   Chuck Klosterman, *Chuck Klosterman IV: A Decade of Curious People and Dangerous Ideas* (New York: Scribner, 2006), 12–20.

5   Steven Daly, "Britney Spears, Teen Queen: *Rolling Stone*'s 1999 Cover Story," *Rolling Stone*, 29 March 2011, http://www.rollingstone.com/music/news/britney-spears-teen-queen-rolling-stones-1999-cover-story-20110329#ixzz3tdTAwIoU.

Run the World

1   Eliza Thompson, "Amber Rose Talks Sex, Stripping, and How the Internet Made Her a 'Feminist Monster,'" *Cosmopolitan*, 8 June 2015, http://www.cosmopolitan.com/entertainment/celebs/a40004/amber-rose-internets-most-fascinating/.

2   Trish Bendix, "Amber Rose Gets Her Own Radio Show, Says Her Sex Life Has Nothing to Do with Her Celebrity," AfterEllen.com, 15 March 2011, http://www.afterellen.com/people/85897-amber-rose-gets-her-ownradio-show-says-her-sex-life-has-nothing-to-do-with-her-celebrity.

All the Lives I Want

1 Sylvia Plath Literature Flats—Made to Order, custombykylee, Etsy, no longer available on Etsy.

2 Sylvia Plath Doll Miniature Art Collectible Author and Writer, UneekDollDesigns, Etsy, https://www.etsy.com/listing /255285639/sylvia-plath-doll-miniature-art?utm_source =google&utm_medium=cpc&utm_campaign=shopping _us_b-art_and_collectibles-collectibles-figurines&utm _custom1=97827bf5-9227-4c29-b917-50c2a43fe284&gclid =CL3QkPDe8MkCFQwjHwod-bkK5g.

3 Marianne Egeland, *Claiming Sylvia Plath: The Poet as Exemplary Figure* (Cambridge: Cambridge Scholars Publishing, 2013).

4 Terry Castle, "The Unbearable," *New York Review of Books*, 11 July 2013, http://www.nybooks.com/articles/2013/07/11 /sylvia-plath-the-unbearable/.

5 Sylvia Plath Ink, Tumblr, http://sylviaplathink.tumblr.com/.

Heavenly Creatures

1 Chris Heath, "Fiona: The Caged Bird Sings," *Rolling Stone*, 22 January 1998, http://www.rollingstone.com/music/news /fiona-the-caged-bird-sings-19980122#ixzz3spITKzJ9.

2 John Calvert, "Original Sin: An Interview with Lana Del Rey," Quietus, 4 October 2011, http://thequietus.com/articles /07106-lana-del-rey-interview.

3 Ibid.

4 Dan P. Lee, "'I Just Want to Feel Everything': Hiding Out with Fiona Apple, Musical Hermit," Vulture, 17 June 2012, http://www.vulture.com/2012/06/hiding-out-with-fiona -apple-musical-hermit.html.

There Can Be Only One

1 "Rare Lil Kim Interview 1996," PhatClips, shown on YouTube, https://www.youtube.com/watch?v=5gTxNhUjs24.

2 Terry Sawyer, "Lil' Kim: Hardcore," *PopMatters*, 20 February 2003, http://www.popmatters.com/review/lilkim-hardcore/.

3 Rob Kemp, "Lil' Kim: Biography," *The New Rolling Stone Album Guide*, 2004, http://web.archive.org/web/20090423133705/http://www.rollingstone.com/artists/lilkim/biography.

4 Greg Thomas, *Hip-Hop Revolution in the Flesh: Power, Knowledge, and Pleasure in Lil' Kim's Lyricism* (New York: Palgrave Macmillan, 2009).

5 Ibid.

6 Ibid.

7 Danyel Smith, "She Got Game: Foxy Brown Wants to Know What's Wrong with Being Sexy and Strong," *Vibe* 6, no. 10 (December–January 1998–1999), 114.

8 Evelyn McDonnell, "Fox on the Run," *Village Voice*, 2 February 1999, http://www.villagevoice.com/music/fox-on-the-run-6422594.

9 John Kennedy, "Opinion: The Real Reason Lil' Kim Is Dissing Nicki Minaj," *Vibe*, 7 August 2014, http://www.vibe.com/2014/08/opinion-real-reason-lil-kim-dissing-nicki-minaj/.

10 Gabriel Williams, "The Fly Discussion: Lil' Kim Takes Shots at Nicki Minaj," SFPL, http://stuffflypeoplelike.com/42323/the-fly-discussion-lil-kim-takes-shots-at-nicki-minaj/.

11 Vanessa Grigoriadis, "The Passion of Nicki Minaj," *New York Times Magazine*, 7 October 2015, http://www.nytimes.com/2015/10/11/magazine/the-passion-of-nicki-minaj.html?_r=1.

12 Ibid.

13 Michael Cragg, "Interview: The Wrath of Lil Kim," *Guardian*, 19 July 2013, http://www.theguardian.com/music/2013/jul/19/lil-kim-interview.

14 Joe Coscarelli, "Miley Cyrus on Nicki Minaj and Hosting a 'Raw' MTV Video Music Awards," *New York Times*, 27 August 2015, http://www.nytimes.com/2015/08/28/arts/music/miley-cyrus-2015-mtv-vmas.html?_r=0.

15 Grigoriadis, "The Passion of Nicki Minaj."

The Queen of Hearts

1 David Fricke, "Hole: *Live Through This*," *Rolling Stone*, 21 April 1994, http://www.rollingstone.com/music/albumreviews/live-through-this-19940421.

2 "25 Seminal Albums from 1994—And What NME Said at the Time," NME, http://www.nme.com/photos/25-seminal-albums-from-1994-and-what-nme-said-at-the-time/330128.

3 Anwen Crawford, *Hole's Live Through This* (New York: Bloomsbury, 2015), 73.

4 Adam Bychawski, "'Live Through This': Not a Hole Lotta Kurt," NME, 16 October 1998, http://www.nme.com/news/courtney-love/634.

5 Tom Breihan, "*Live Through This* Turns 20," *StereoGum*, 11 April 2014, http://www.stereogum.com/1675044/live-through-this-turns-20/franchises/the-anniversary/.

6 Alex Galbraith, "Why I Think Hole Is a Better Band Than Nirvana (No, Really, I'm Not Trolling)," UPROXX, 9 July 2015, http://uproxx.com/music/hole-vs-nirvana/.

7 Greg Fisher, "Lawsuit to Release Graphic Kurt Cobain Death Photos Thrown Out," CBS News, 31 July 2015, http://www .cbsnews.com/news/lawsuit-to-release-graphic-kurt-cobain -death-photos-thrown-out/.

8 Kevin Sessums, "Love Child," *VF News*, June 1995, http:// www.vanityfair.com/news/1995/06/courtney-love-199506.

9 Poppy Z. Brite, *Courtney Love: The Real Story* (New York: Touchstone, 1997), 25.

10 Sessums, "Love Child."

11 Craig Marks, "Endless Love," *Spin*, February 1995, 47.

12 Brite, *Courtney Love*, 27.

13 Charles R. Cross, "The Moment Kurt Cobain Met Courtney Love," Daily Beast, 5 April 2015, http://www.thedailybeast.com /articles/2014/03/04/the-moment-kurt-cobain-met-courtney -love.html.

14 "Love Conquers All," *Spin*, May 1994, 39.

15 Brenna Ehrlich, "Michael Stipe Recalls Meeting Kurt Cobain— and His Blue Eyes," *MTV News*, 11 April 2014, http://www .mtv.com/news/1725948/nirvana-michael-stipe-st-vincent -rock-hall-of-fame/.

16 "Cobain: Montage of Heck," IMDB, http://www.imdb.com /title/tt4229236/.

17 Crawford, *Hole's Live Through This*, 19.

18 Owen Davies, *Witchcraft, Magic and Culture 1736–1951* (Manchester: Manchester University Press, 1999), 174.

19 Sessums, "Love Child."

NOTES

Charlotte in Exile

1 *Lost in Translation*, http://www.lost-in-translation.com/.

2 Peter Travers, "*Lost in Translation*," *Rolling Stone*, 8 September 2003, http://www.rollingstone.com/movies/reviews/lost-in -translation-20030908.

3 Elvis Mitchell, "Film Review; An American in Japan, Making a Connection," *New York Times*, 12 September 2003, http://www.nytimes.com/movie/review?res=9803E1D8133B F931A2575AC0A9659C8B63.

4 Peter Rainer, "Sleepless in Tokyo," *New York* magazine, http:// nymag.com/nymetro/movies/reviews/n_9178/.

5 Roger Ebert, "*Lost in Translation*," 12 September 2003, http:// www.rogerebert.com/reviews/lost-in-translation-2003.

6 "Scarlett Johansson Takes Two HIV Tests a Year but Says She's Not Promiscuous," *Daily Mail*, 10 October 2006, http://www .dailymail.co.uk/tvshowbiz/article-409657/Scarlett-Johansson -takes-HIV-tests-year-says-shes-promiscuous.html.

7 Ava Cadell, "Mystery Behind Scarlett's AIDS Tests," *Globe*, 6 November 2006, https://www.avacadell.com/magazines -press/globe/324-scarlett-johanson.

8 Tom Chiarella, "Scarlett Johansson Is 2013's Sexiest Woman Alive," *Esquire*, http://www.esquire.com/entertainment /a25017/scarlett-johansson-interview-1113/.

9 Nick Clark, "Novel Scarlett Johansson Tried to Ban, Grégoire Delacourt's *The First Thing You See*, to Be Published in UK," *Independent*, 26 August 2015, http://www .independent.co.uk/arts-entertainment/books/news/novel -scarlett-johansson-tried-to-ban-gr-goire-delacourt-s-the-first -thing-you-see-to-be-published-10473492.html.

No She Without Her

1 "Mary-Kate Olsen Breaks Her Silence," *Marie Claire*, 4 August 2010, http://www.marieclaire.com/celebrity/a5174/mary-kate -olsen-interview/.

2 Marshall Heyman, "Mary-Kate Olsen," *W*, January 2006, http://www.wmagazine.com/culture/film-and-tv/2006/01 /mary_kate_olsen/.

3 "Ashley or Mary-Kate?" TheEllenShow, 24 April 2014, https:// www.youtube.com/watch?v=APshm-9gPgI.

4 "Mary-Kate Olsen Breaks Her Silence," *Marie Claire*.

American Pain

1 Caryn James, "Critic's Notebook; Reality Shows as Sideshows," 6 August 2002, http://www.nytimes.com/2002/08/06/arts /critic-s-notebook-reality-shows-as-sideshows.html.

2 Steve Johnson, "Anna Nicole Smith: Larger Than Life," *Chicago Tribune*, 2 August 2002, http://articles.chicagotribune .com/2002-08-02/features/0208020004_1_anna-nicole -show-osbournes-tv-critics.

3 Ken Tucker, "Anna Nicole Smith's TV Show Is an Obscene Train Wreck," *Entertainment Weekly*, 5 August 2002, http:// www.ew.com/article/2002/08/05/anna-nicole-smiths-tv -show-obscene-train-wreck.

4 Linda Deutsch, "Doctor Testifies That Anna Nicole Smith Had Chronic Pain Syndrome," *USA Today*, 11 August 2010, http://usatoday30.usatoday.com/life/people/2010-08-11 -smith-trial-wednesday_N.htm.

5 Donna Hogan, *Train Wreck: The Life and Death of Anna Nicole Smith* (Vermont: Phoenix Books, 2007), http://www.amazon

.com/Train-Wreck-Death-Nicole-Smith/dp/1597775401, page 22.

6 Julia Hoffer, "*The Anna Nicole Show* Season 1: Episode 8 Cousin Shelly," YouTube, 5 August 2014, https://www.you tube.com/watch?v=0F3jAkTqfqU.

7 Sue Anne Pressley, "From Courting to Court: A Love Story," *Washington Post*, 7 September 1995, http://articles.latimes .com/1995-09-07/news/ls-42962_1_anna-nicole-smith/2.

8 Dan P. Lee, "Paw Paw & Lady Love," *New York* magazine, 5 June 2011, http://nymag.com/news/features/anna-nicole -smith-2011-6/index1.html.

9 "Anna Nicole Smith's Mother Speaks Out," *Nancy Grace*, 12 October 2006, http://transcripts.cnn.com/TRAN-SCRIPTS/0610/12/ng.01.html.

10 Chelsea White, " 'I Don't Sugar Coat It': Anna Nicole Smith's Ex Larry Birkhead Reveals What He Tells Daughter Dannielynn Now She Is Old Enough to Google Her Mom," *Daily Mail*, 4 November 2015, http://www.dailymail.co.uk /tvshowbiz/article-3303874/Anna-Nicole-Smith-s-ex-Larry-Birkhead-reveals-tells-daughter-Dannielynn-old-Google-mom .html.

A Bigger Fairy Tale

1 Ben Brantley, "Anjelica—Solo," *Vanity Fair*, July 1990, http:// www.vanityfair.com/news/1990/07/anjelica-huston-jack -nicholson.

2 Ibid.

3 Brad Darrach, "Jack Finds His Queen of Hearts," *People*, 8 July 1985, http://www.people.com/people/archive/article /0,,20091237,00.html.

4 Anjelica Huston, "Nostalgia: Anjelica Huston Remembers the Richard Avedon Photograph That Launched Her Career," *Vogue*, 19 November 2013, http://www.vogue.com/865182 /nostalgia-anjelica-huston-remembers-the-richard-avedon -photograph-that-launched-her-career/.

5 Durga Chew-Bose, "Things That Ordinary People Wouldn't Do: To Die For at 20," Hazlitt, 3 December 2015, http://hazlitt .net/longreads/things-ordinary-people-wouldnt-do-die-20.

6 Anjelica Huston, *A Story Lately Told: Coming of Age in Ireland, London, and New York* (New York: Scribner, 2013), https://books.google.com/books?id=4NO5BAAAQBAJ&pg= PA261&lpg=PA261&dq=Diana+Vreeland+was+to+christen +it,+%E2%80%98The+Killer+Smile.%E2%80%99+But+at +the+time+I+thought,+%E2%80%98Ah!+Yes.+Now,+there %E2%80%99s+a+man+you+could+fall+for.%E2%80%99& source=bl&ots=gB-eqfvqfO&sig= 4jh0hpRkAiC6NPKceRvS _z2Tn GA&hl = en &sa =X&ved = 0ahUKEwjRuPWs6I LNAhVEXB4KHfxfCAkQ6AEIHTA A#v=onepage&q=Diana %20Vreeland%20was%20to%20christen%20it%2C%20 %E2%80%98The%20Killer%20Smile.%E2%80%99%20 But%20at%20the%20time%20I%20thought%2C%20% E2%80%98Ah!%20Yes.%20Now%2C% 20 there%E2%80%99s%20a%20man%20you%20could%20 fall%20for.%E2%80%99&f=false.

7 Darrach, "Jack Finds His Queen of Hearts."

8 Anjelica Huston, *Watch Me* (New York: Scribner, 2014), 33.

9 Huston, *Watch Me*, 107.

10 Darrach, "Jack Finds His Queen of Hearts."

11 Brantley, "Anjelica—Solo."

12 Huston, *Watch Me*, https://books.google.com/books?id=8t KbAwAAQBAJ&pg=PP148&lpg=PP148&dq=These+pearls+

from+your+swine.+With+happiest+wishes+for+the+holi
days%E2%80%94Enjoy%E2%80%94Yr+Jack,
&source=bl&ots=xSO5e8Jta3&sig=   WMxjiPAH2l9b2ZW
-jFDlKPAUQxo&hl=en&sa=X&ved=0ahUKEwj5_Zv36
ILNAhXJ7R4KHSl9B6cQ6AEIHTAA#v=onep age&q=These
%20pearls%20from%20your%20swine.%20With%20happi
est%20wishes%20for%20the%20holidays%E2%80%94En
joy%E2%80%94Yr%20Jack%2C&f=false.

13 Marc Eliot, *Nicholson: A Biography* (New York: Random House,
    2013), https://books.google.com/books?id=oHjEZ15cSgIC&
    pg=PT287&lpg=PT287&dq=anjelica+huston+hots+up
    &source=bl&ots=DBbaB5uaiZ&sig=nEfFtLQs
    -pKDM4hfaK-nUtolcas&hl=en&sa=X&ved=0ahUKE
    wiVk_yNrvDJAhXGrD4KHbdKA5UQ6AEIRDAJ#v=one
    page&q=anjelica%20huston%20hots%20up&f=false.

14 Brantley, "Anjelica—Solo."

15 Huston, *Watch Me*, 234.

16 Huston, *Watch Me*, 361.

17 John Heilpern, "Guardian Anjelica," *VF News*, February
    2010, http://www.vanityfair.com/news/2010/02/out-to-lunch
    -huston-201002.

18 "Jack Nicholson Fears He'll End Up Alone After a Lifetime
    of Chasing Beautiful Women," *Closer Weekly*, 10 January
    2015,   http://www.closerweekly.com/posts/jack-nicholson
    -fears-he-ll-end-up-alone-after-a-lifetime-of-chasing-beautiful
    -women-49265.

Long-Game Bitches

1 Tina Brown, "Diana's Final Heartbreak," *VF News*, July 2007,
   http://www.vanityfair.com/news/2007/07/diana200707.

2 Ibid.

3 Sasha Goldstein, "Lorena Bobbitt Has Longtime Partner, Daughter and Domestic Abuse Charity Two Decades After Cutting Off John Wayne Bobbitt's Penis," *New York Daily News*, 29 April 2014, http://www.nydailynews.com/news/national/lorena-bobbitt-moved-decades-cutting-john-bobbitt-penis-article-1.1773382.

4 "Interview with TLC's Left Eye," *Sister 2 Sister*, February 1998, http://www.geocities.ws/ladylefteye/s2sinterview.html.

5 Ibid.

6 Ibid.

7 Hazel Cills, "Why 2014 Was the Year of the 'Crazy Ex-Girl friend,'" *Pitchfork*, 12 November 2014, http://pitchfork.com/thepitch/549-why-2014-was-the-year-of-the-crazy-ex-girlfriend/.

8 Nancy Jo Sales and Jessica Diehl, "Taylor Swift's Telltale Heart," *Vanity Fair*, April 2013, http://www.vanityfair.com/hollywood/2013/04/taylor-swift-cover-story.

9 Ryan O'Connell, "Taylor Swift Is a Psycho," Thought Catalog, 25 October 2012, http://thoughtcatalog.com/ryan-oconnell/2012/10/taylor-swift-is-a-psycho/.

10 "John Mayer: Taylor Swift's 'Dear John' Song 'Humiliated Me,'" *Rolling Stone*, 6 June 2012, http://www.rollingstone.com/music/news/john-mayer-taylor-swifts-dear-john-song-humiliated-me-20120606.

11 Maureen O'Connor, "'My Career Is Over': Another Terrifying Mel Gibson Phone Call Is Now Online," *Gawker*, 12 July 2010, http://gawker.com/5584987/my-career-is-over-another-terrifying-mel-gibson-phone-call-is-now-online.

12 "'Of Course I Feel Regret...but I Was Betrayed': Mel Gibson Opens Up for First Time About Oksana Tape Recordings," *Daily Mail*, 22 April 2011, http://www.dailymail.co.uk /tvshowbiz/article-1379492/Mel-Gibson-opens-Oksana-Grig orieva-tape-recordings-1st-time.html.

13 Mark, "Mel Gibson Has Had Better Weekends," *Gawker*, 31 July 2006, http://gawker.com/190848/mel-gibson-has-had -better-weekends.

14 "Gibson Skated Twice Before," *TMZ*, 31 July 2006, http:// www.tmz.com/2006/07/31/exclusive-gibson-skated-two -times-before/.

15 Maureen O'Connor, "All the Terrible Things Mel Gibson Has Said on the Record," *Gawker*, 8 July 2010, http://gawker.com/5582644 /all-the-terrible-things-mel-gibson-has-said-on-the-record.

16 Ibid.

17 Peter J. Boyer, "The Jesus War," *New Yorker*, 15 September 2003, http://www.newyorker.com/magazine/2003/09/15/the -jesus-war.

18 "Robyn Gibson Supports Mel in Court," *TMZ*, 15 July 2010, http://www.tmz.com/2010/07/15/mel-gibson-robyn-gibson -declaration-domestic-violence-court-filed/.

19 Katie Kindelan via *Good Morning America*, "Mel Gibson Loses Half of His $850 Million Fortune to Ex-Wife in Divorce," ABC News, http://abcnews.go.com/blogs/entertainment/2011/12/mel- gibsons-loses-half-of-his-850-million-fortune-to-ex-wife-in -divorce/.

Emparadised

1 Meghan Daum, "The Elitist Allure of Joan Didion," *Atlantic*, September 2015, http://www.theatlantic.com/magazine/archive/2015/09/the-elitist-allure-of-joan-didion/399320/.

2 Haley Mlotek, "Free Joan Didion," The Awl, 13 January 2015, https://theawl.com/free-joan-didion-12e21fc4d6d6#.oyla1rnt8.

About the Author

Alana Massey is a writer whose work covers culture, identity, vice, and virtue. She is presently at work cultivating all four in her personal time. Massey's essays, criticism, reviews, and reporting appear regularly in publications like *The Guardian*, *New York Magazine*, *Elle*, Hazlitt, The New Inquiry, BuzzFeed, and more, while photos of herself and her cat, Keith, can be found primarily on Twitter and nefarious men's rights blog posts. Massey splits her time between New York City and Saugerties, New York, where she indulges her passions for books, cats, champagne, and glitter. Only occasionally all at once.